FAULKNER'S REVISION OF *SANCTUARY*

Faulkner's Revision of *Sanctuary*

A Collation of the Unrevised Galleys and the Published Book

by GERALD LANGFORD

UNIVERSITY OF TEXAS PRESS

AUSTIN

For Nancy

CONTENTS

ACKNOWLEDGMENTS

Grateful acknowledgment is made to Random House, Inc., for permission to quote from *Sanctuary*, by William Faulkner. Copyright 1931 and renewed 1959 by William Faulkner. Acknowledgment is also made to Curtis Brown Ltd. who holds the British rights.

Thanks are due also to Yale University Press for permission to quote from *William Faulkner: The Yoknapatawpha Country*, by Cleanth Brooks (copyright 1963 by Yale University); and to the Bibliographical Society of Virginia, for permission to quote from "Notes on the Unrevised Galleys of Faulkner's *Sanctuary*," by Linton Massey, in *Studies in Bibliography* 7 (1956).

FAULKNER'S REVISION OF *SANCTUARY*

Introduction

The doubtful value of authors' statements about the intended purposes or meanings of their works has rarely been more clearly illustrated than by the comments Faulkner made about his most popularly successful novel. In 1932, the year after *Sanctuary* was first published, he wrote:

> This book was written three years ago. To me it is a cheap idea, because it was deliberately conceived to make money. I had been writing books for about five years, which got published and not bought. . . . I began to think of books in terms of possible money. I decided I might just as well make some of it myself. I took a little time out, and speculated what a person in Mississippi would believe to be current trends, chose what I thought was the right answer and invented the most horrific tale I could imagine and wrote it in about three weeks and sent it to Smith, who had done *The Sound and the Fury* and who wrote me immediately, "Good God, I can't publish this. We'd both be in jail." So I told Faulkner, "You're damned. You'll have to work now and then for the rest of your life. . . ."
>
> I think I had forgotten about *Sanctuary*, just as you might forget about anything made for an immediate purpose, which did not come off. *As I Lay Dying* was published and I didn't remember the mss. of *Sanctuary* until Smith sent me the galleys. Then I saw that it was so terrible that there were but two things to do: tear it up or rewrite it. I thought again, "It might sell; maybe 10,000 of them will buy it." So I tore the galleys down and rewrote the book. It had been already set up once, so I had to pay for the privilege of rewriting it, trying to make out of it something which would not shame *The Sound and the Fury* and *As I Lay Dying* too much and I made a fair job and I hope you will buy it and tell your friends and I hope they will buy it too.[1]

Some critics have interpreted Faulkner's disparagement not as a comment on *Sanctuary* so much as a contemptuous slap at readers who had neglected his work until they found in it what they took to be meretricious

---

[1] Introduction to the Modern Library edition of *Sanctuary*, 1932, pp. v, vi, vii. Twenty-five years later, when asked whether he would repudiate his earlier estimate of the book, Faulkner declined to do so. " 'Well,' he said, 'that book was basely conceived. I had written and had never made much money, and I—when I was footloose I could do things to make money—I could run a bootlegging boat, I was a commercial airplane pilot—things like that—then I got married and I couldn't do things like that anymore,

sensationalism. Other critics, while accepting at face value the disparagement of the novel as first written, have judged the revised *Sanctuary* to be a considerably more significant book than Faulkner himself believed it to be. It was not until 1956, with the publication of Linton Massey's brief article, "Notes on the Unrevised Galleys of Faulkner's *Sanctuary*," that the original version of the novel was publicly known to have survived in several sets of galley proofs. Having gained access to one of these sets and compared it with the published version, Mr. Massey undertook to confirm the truthfulness of Faulkner's account of the composition and revision of the book.

According to Mr. Massey, Faulkner did indeed make drastic changes in a story that "surely revealed carelessness and disclosed a lamentable dichotomy in purpose. . . . Actually, there were two stories in these pages of galley proof, the Freudian study of Horace Benbow in the one; and in the other, the adventures of Temple Drake, an inquiry into the nature of sin as one facet in that trinity of the ritualism of re-birth: sin, suffering, and salvation." Further evidences of confusion are to be found, we are told, in the "multiple and often inexplicable shifts in time and locale . . . to say nothing of a further contribution made to disorder and general untidiness by frequent alterations in the point of view, from that of the author himself to one or another of the characters, and back again." Finally, there is the matter of "the excrescences, those passages which delayed the action without serving it, such as, for instance, that episode transplanted in full bloom out of *Sartoris* depicting Horace's affair with Belle while she was still married to her first husband, Harry Mitchell." Thus, Mr. Massey concludes, in the process of revision

> Faulkner altered the entire focus and meaning of the book; he simplified a too-complex structure; he excluded the irrelevant; he clarified the obscure passages where ambiguity was not an asset; he amplified those portions

---

and so I thought I would make a little money writing a book. And I thought of the most horrific idea I could think of and wrote it. I sent it to the publisher, and he wrote me back and said, Good Lord, if we print this, we'll both be in jail. That was about 192—
—about 1930, I think, when you couldn't say things in print like you can now. So I forgot it, I wrote two more books, they were published, and then one day I got the galleys for *Sanctuary* and I read it and—probably it was because I didn't need money so badly then, but anyway I saw what a base thing it was in concept, what a shabby thing it was and so I wrote the publisher and said, Let's throw it away. He didn't have much money at the time and he said, We can't do that because I've had plates made and that costs something. And I said, Well, I'll just have to rewrite it. And he said, All right, you rewrite it and I'll pay half of the new plates and you pay half of the new plates. So I rewrote it, did the best I could with it. I got a job passing coal to earn the $270 to pay my half for the plates to print the book and then the publisher went bankrupt. I didn't get any money at all. So I did the best I could with the book. It was in a way already in the public domain, I couldn't throw it away and I rewrote it and did the best I could with it . . .'' (*Faulkner in the University*, Frederick L. Gwynn and Joseph L. Blotner [New York: Vintage Books, 1965], p. 90).

requiring emendation; he gave the novel a climax; and he freed it from its bonds of previous servitude to an earlier book.

For the magnitude of his accomplishment there can be only admiration; for the skill he revealed there can be only respect; and for his minor miracle of revision there can be only gratitude. Had he failed, had he served up in error that mishmash of Freudianism out of day-before-yesterday's scraps, then it is possible to believe he might at the same time have committed the artistic suicide he once mentioned when, long ago, out of sheer desperation, he took refuge in the writing of a book with the magnificently ironic title of *Sanctuary*.[2]

Since this verdict was rendered fifteen years ago, Faulkner's own corrected set of galleys has become available for examination at The University of Texas at Austin, as have another set of galleys and the handwritten manuscript and a carbon typescript at the University of Virginia. Yet except for Michael Millgate's brief comments on Faulkner's revision of the novel, the matter has rested where Mr. Massey left it. Mr. Millgate makes the significant point that critics still assume the "horrific" elements of the original version to be the basis of Faulkner's repudiation of it as a cheap idea, whereas the fact is "that the extensive deletions made by Faulkner in no instance included anything that might be described as especially violent or 'horrific.' " As a whole, however, the Millgate appraisal of the revisions is in substantial agreement with the Massey appraisal: "What must strike the reader [of the original novel] . . . is how badly it is put together . . . : the slackness and loose proliferation of the Benbow material had produced narrative confusion in the opening chapters and a persistent failure of dramatic tension culminating, as we have seen, in the clumsy exchange of letters at the point where the published book has the climactic scene of the lynching of Goodwin and the threatened lynching of Horace himself."[3]

It is such an appraisal which the generalized observations of the two commentators leave open to question. Before we can satisfactorily judge whether *Sanctuary* was a careless potboiler turned into a respectable book through reworking, we need a detailed examination of the two texts. In the collation that follows, a reader with the published text before him can reconstruct the original version for himself, simultaneously noting the cancellations, the additions, and the rewritten passages. It will facilitate matters to have a preliminary acquaintance with the story as it was first written.

Instead of beginning with Horace's pause at the Old Frenchmans place on his way to Jefferson, Chapter I in the galleys opened three weeks after

[2]Linton Massey, "Notes on the Unrevised Galleys of Faulkner's *Sanctuary*," *Studies in Bibliography* 7 (1956): 195–208.

[3]Michael Millgate, *The Achievement of William Faulkner* (New York: Random House, 1965), pp. 115, 116, 117.

Goodwin's arrest for the murder of Tommy. During the lull before the trial Horace was reminded of the night of the arrest, when he had agreed to take the case and had installed Ruby in the Benbow family house, only to reconsider and move Ruby to the hotel in submission to Narcissa's protest and Miss Jenny's hint that he might be suspected of collusion with his client. (In succeeding chapters the background of Horace's involvement in the case was supplied through a long series of flashbacks, during which the time sequence became so uncertain that it is not clear at what point the narrative again picked up the present time established in the beginning—that is, three weeks after Goodwin's arrest on May 12, the day of the murder (see *Sanctuary*, p. 278).[4]

Chapter II began with a flashback to the afternoon in Kinston when Horace caught the mirrored glimpse of Little Belle's dissimulation. Then, in a flashback within a flashback, the scene shifted to a conversation at the time of Horace's courtship of Belle, who had taunted him with the accusation that he was in love with his sister, after which the scene shifted to his unsuccessful attempt to dissuade Narcissa from marrying Bayard Sartoris. Returning to the day of Horace's talk with Little Belle (the same day he decided to leave his wife), the narrative progressed as far as his encounter with Popeye and the evening he spent at Goodwin's home.

In Chapter III, in a flashback to the day he was cleaning up his family home (to which he had moved back after taking Ruby to the hotel), Horace had a visit from the disapproving Narcissa, a scene that led backward to Gowan Stevens's visit to Narcissa some days earlier, just before Gowan's weekend date with Temple Drake. After the young man departed, Horace tried to explain to Narcissa and Miss Jenny his reasons for agreeing to act as Goodwin's lawyer—a subject that in Chapter IV prompted another flashback to the evening he had spent at Goodwin's home, where he was now shown to have felt a strong sexual attraction toward Ruby.

Chapter V dealt with the two days Horace spent at Narcissa's home when he first arrived in Jefferson. His break with his wife motivated several flashbacks to scenes involving his mother, his sister, and his stepdaughter. Finally he decided to move to his long-unoccupied family home in town, and and on the following day he happened to pass the undertaker's parlor where Tommy's murdered body lay.

In Chapter VI Horace moved, for the sake of convenience, back out to Narcissa's home, where he read the farewell letter to Narcissa from Gowan Stevens after the latter's humiliating experience with Temple Drake. Horace responded to a call from Ruby, who confided that a girl had been present on the night Tommy was murdered. This disclosure was followed in Chapter VII by a flashback to the weekend when Gowan took Temple to the Old Frenchman place to buy whisky from Goodwin. Continuing the flashback,

---

[4]Page references to the published text are to the new Modern Library edition (1966). The still more recent Vintage paperback edition is printed from the same plates.

Chapters VIII and IX dealt with Temple's frightening evening at Goodwin's house, and, after a brief return to the scene of Ruby's narration to Horace, Chapters X and XI completed the account of the murder and the rape.

In Chapter XII, after Ruby finished her account of Popeye's departure with Temple, Horace went to Oxford in a vain search for Temple as a possible witness in court. That night, after meeting Clarence Snopes on the return train, he learned that Ruby had been forced to leave the hotel where she had been staying.

Chapters XIII, XIV, and XV were devoted to a long flashback to Temple's trip to Memphis with Popeye. He installed her in Miss Reba's house, where, in Chapter XVI, Virgil and Fonzo became lodgers. Apparently it was at this point that the narrative picked up the present time of the novel, three weeks after Goodwin's arrest.

In Chapter XVII Horace moved from Narcissa's home back to town to prepare for the trial. He found Ruby a shelter and paid Clarence Snopes for information about Temple's whereabouts. In Chapter XVIII he visited Temple at Miss Reba's, after which, in the three following chapters, there was an account of Temple's relationship with Red and then the scene of Red's grotesque funeral. Chapter XXII was concerned with Horace's preparations for the trial and Narcissa's betrayal of his plan to the district attorney. The trial itself occupied the next two chapters, ending with Temple's perjury, which was the climax of the original novel. The aftermath was sketched in three brief chapters. Chapter XXV consisted of a letter in which Horace, having returned to Belle, asked Narcissa to notify Ruby that the case would be appealed by the best criminal lawyer he could find. In reply (Chapter XXVI), Narcissa reported that Goodwin had been moved from Jefferson because of the threat of a lynching. In the final chapter Popeye was hanged for a crime he had not committed (there was no account of his parents and his childhood), and Temple was glimpsed with her father in the Luxembourg Gardens.

As even this bald summary suggests, the original version of *Sanctuary* was no more horrific than the published book, and a detailed comparison reveals that none of the passages that might be questioned by a censor were altered in the revision. Indeed, far from reworking a lurid sex story into a more significant work, Faulkner seems to have had a single practical purpose—to turn a slow-moving psychological study into a streamlined drama ready for the cameras of Hollywood. The intricate pattern of flashbacks and shifting perspectives was discarded for a chronological presentation that plays down the impact of events on Horace and thus highlights the sensationalism of the story of Temple Drake. Though the original narrative was grievously disappointing in its resolution, it possessed a depth of texture that was flattened in the reworking. Moreover, the changes made by Faulkner surely had an effect just the opposite of remedying what Mr. Massey calls a dichotomy of purpose. Unlike the revised version (which, as Edmond L. Volpe has correctly pointed out,[5] is marred by a structural split between two central characters), the story as Faulkner first wrote it was unmistakably focused on Horace as the protagonist.

In the published novel the first three chapters (twenty-seven pages) are told from Horace's point of view, but the seventy-page section devoted to Temple is told from her point of view; we lose sight of Horace completely, and even after his return in Chapter XV we continue to lose sight of him and concern ourselves primarily with Temple. In the galleys, however, Horace dominated the first six chapters, and Temple's experiences with Popeye were then presented in flashbacks which repeatedly emphasized the fact that Horace was remembering the story as told by Ruby. This structural device to keep Horace in the foreground was supplemented by numerous passages, cut in revision, that kept the spotlight on him. For example, in Horace's first encounter with Popeye at the spring, the dialogue was interrupted by a passage that emphasized not the drama of the moment but the later significance of the encounter for Horace: "Later—much later, it was—the woman—she was sitting on the bed in the hotel, beside the child. It had been really sick this time and it lay rigid beneath the blanket, its arms spread in an attitude of utter exhaustion, its eyelids less than half closed, breathing with a thin, whistling sound while Horace looked down at it, marvelling at the pertinacity with which it clung to the breath which was destroying it.—The woman said: 'If I had my way, I'd hang every man that makes whiskey or sells it or drinks it, every God's one of them' " (see Collation, p. 49).

Again, when Popeye led Horace from the spring to the Goodwin's house, the following description was included:

> Three men were sitting on the porch. The woman wasn't there. It never occurred to Horace that there would be a woman there; there was that about the bleak ruin which precluded femininity. It was like coming upon one of those antediluvian thighbones or ribcages which flout credulity by its very fragmentary majesty and from which they reconstruct an organization too grandly executed to have housed such trivial things as comfort and happiness and nagging and affection. As though whatever women had dwelled there had been no more than a part of the vanished pageantry of a dream; in their hoops and crinoline but the lost puppets of someone's pomp and pride, moldering peacefully now in a closet somewhere, surrounded by a faint shattering of dried and odorless petals, leaving not so much as the print of a slipper on the dusty stage. Since he had last seen it they had chopped down two of the pillars on the portico with axes, and there was a walnut newel post six feet tall and a balustrade without a single spindle left. It went half way up the wall, then it just ceased. Vanished, steps and all, leaving a faded imprint of stairs mounting the wall in ghostly progression,

---

[5]Edmond L. Volpe, *A Reader's Guide to William Faulkner* (New York: Farrar, Strauss and Giroux, 1964), p. 143.

and in one room was a marble fireplace with the scrolled frame of an eight foot pier glass, with a few fragments of blackened mirror in the corners of the frame. (See Collation, p. 75)

This was not a needlessly detailed and thus dispensable account of the house. It told the reader something about Horace's feeling for women and his feeling for the past, both of which were important elements in a personality more complex and more interesting in the galleys than in the published book. Later, at the supper table, the quality of Horace's sensitivity was further revealed in another canceled passage: "And while he was watching her [Ruby's] hands he felt the thug looking at him and he raised his eyes and saw that the man had no eyelashes at all, and when he blinked something seemed to move laterally across his eyeballs, like an owl's, and Horace thought, Fancy being killed by a man you didn't know had no eyelashes, feeling the man's naked-looking eyes upon him as bits of soft rubber, thinking fretfully, You'd think there'd have to be a kinship between two people who looked on death at the same time, even though it was from opposite sides" (see Collation, p. 76). When Tommy was introduced, it was his effect on Horace which was emphasized in the galleys: "He had a beautiful face, with pale eyes and a soft young beard like dirty gold. Like Christ he looked: a sort of rapt, furious face. Horace thought of form without substance, like the jet of a plumber's torch under a spell, reft of all motion and heat. He was barefoot. Horace could hear his feet on the floor, hissing a little, and whenever he drank from the jug Horace could hear them scouring slowly in an innocent and prolonged orgasm" (see Collation, p. 76).

As Faulkner originally interwove the story of Temple into the novel, he provided frequent glimpses of the effect of the shocking events on Horace. For example, after Horace had heard Ruby's account of Temple's presence at the time Tommy was murdered, he looked differently at "the shady lawns and houses—all the stability which he had known always—a stage upon which tragedy kept to a certain predictableness, decorum. Of course she's all right, he said. She's down there at school now. Probably just gotten over being thoroughly scared, damn her. Damn her. . . . 'Of course she's all right,' he said. 'Things like that dont happen'" (see Collation, p. 98). Later, in Oxford, where Horace went to seek Temple, he tried again to dissociate himself from the situation in which he had become involved: "Watching them [the throngs of college girls] Horace began to laugh, without mirth. And this is what I have been losing sleep over, he thought. What can a creature like that suffer, else where the dignity in tragedy—that one quality which we do not possess in common with the beasts of the field, standing there in the bright dappling of noon, thinking that she might have been the very one who forced him to step off the walk in order to pass her: the supreme gesture of that irony which ordered his life" (see Collation, p. 104). Another example is a passage dealing with Horace's attempt to come to terms with the violent impact of his talk with Temple at Miss Reba's house:

> Looking about him he saw his life isolated in all its ludicrous and optimistic frustration; looking ahead he could see it diminishing into a small frenzied dust where he strove with the subterfuge and prejudice and lying, to no end. What did it matter who killed the man? what became of Goodwin, of her, of a fool little girl, of himself? All that matters is to accomplish what is at hand, clean up the mess he had got himself into, then be forever afterward as fearful as any buck of the scent or sight or sound of collective man. . . . Not that it mattered whether they hung Goodwin or not, any more than it mattered whether or not Tommy was dead. Telling the jury What ever you do will be as stupid as what has been done, but just do something, because he was sick to death. Then suddenly, passing a house, he smelled coffee, and he knew he could not do that. He went to the hotel and with knife and fork he dug himself back into that world he had vomited himself out of for a time, in which he must follow a certain ordered procedure about which he had neither volition nor will. (See Collation, p. 110)

The passages Faulkner omitted in revision did not serve merely to keep Horace in the foreground of the original novel. In addition, they clarified the personality of Horace and made him a more understandable character than the somewhat implausible idealist he becomes in the revised version. Notable, for example, is a series of passages emphasizing his response to Ruby's sexual attraction:

> It was after midnight when he left the house with the barefooted man. He found that he was drunker than he had thought, as though some quality in the darkness, the silence, the steady motion of walking, had released the alcohol which the woman, her presence, consciousness of her voice, her flesh, had held for the time in abeyance. (See Collation, p. 52)

> When she first came into the room he thought she was just another hill-woman, just another of those hopeless, malaria-ridden women he could see, barefoot, with a snuff-stick in her mouth and half a dozen children peeping around her skirts, in any cabin door. But there was something about her, something of that abject arrogance, that mixture of arrogance and cringing beneath all the lace and scent which he had felt when the inmates of brothels entered the parlor in the formal parade of shrill identical smiles through which the old lusts and the old despairs peeped; something that so definitely postulated her femaleness, as though from long and weary habit. Not the fact that she belonged to that nagging disturbing inescapable half of the race, but that she was a vessel about which lingered an aura of past pleasures and a reaffirmation of future pleasures of superior, if automatic, sort. (See Collation, p. 72)

> "Oh," the woman said. He could hear the deep, slow movement of her bosom, her face still a blur against the dark wall. (See Collation, p. 80)

> Just inside the door the woman stood; he could feel her there: a steady postulate of female flesh with which he was trying to establish that dumb

spark of the universal truth which each man carries inside the slowly hardening shell of his secret breath, into a solitary grave. (See Collation, p. 89)

Deep full her bosom moved under the gray crepe. Horace watched her, the down-turned cheek, the hair bobbed once but drawn now to a knot at the back, at one rigid arm and the slow clenching of her hands in her lap. (See Collation, p. 94)

These passages helped to illuminate a side of Horace's personality that the revised text leaves in shadow, so obscured that some commentators have found Horace a flat character, a mere type. Dorothy Tuck, for example, points out what she considers a major weakness in the novel: "Its characters tend to be two-dimensional and sometimes nearly allegorical figures. . . . Horace Benbow is the good but inept man who is unable to match the forces of evil in the world."[6] Lawrance Thompson also discusses Horace's "well-meaning and yet cowardly" performance as a lawyer: "He has evidence enough to break the case wide-open, and he never tries to use it. He does not even appeal the case. Why? . . . In the trial scene, Horace's passivity baffles even the judge."[7] The reason, Mr. Thompson suggests, is simply that Horace is a familiar type of person—the dodger of moral responsibility, the self-excuser. This lack of sharp individualization resulted from Faulkner's elimination of several aspects of the personality he had originally portrayed. One such aspect is Horace's sexual response to Ruby. As a result of this particular omission, a reader of the published novel must take at face value Horace's repudiation of Ruby's offer of payment for his legal services: " 'You said tonight was the time to start paying you.' For a while longer he looked at her. 'Ah,' he said. 'O tempora! O mores! O hell! Can you stupid mammals never believe that any man, every man— You thought that was what I was coming for? You thought that if I had intended to, I'd have waited this long?' . . . She looked at him, her eyes grave and blank and contemplative. Outside the clock struck twelve. 'Good God,' he whispered. 'What kind of men have you known?' " (*Sanctuary*, pp. 267–268).

In the original conception of the novel, Horace the high-minded idealist turned out, himself, to be one of the kind of men Ruby has known. His sexuality had had to be repressed below the level of his own awareness, however, because it had involved incestuous feelings toward his sister. Such feelings are entirely eliminated from the final version of *Sanctuary*, and it seems hardly legitimate on the part of some commentators to assume their existence because of certain hints in the earlier novel *Sartoris*.

[6]Dorothy Tuck, *Crowell's Handbook of Faulkner* (New York: Thomas Y. Crowell Company, 1964), p. 143.

[7]Lawrance Thompson, *William Faulkner: An Introduction and Interpretation* (New York: Holt, Rinehart and Winston, 1967), p. 108.

Cleanth Brooks, for example, in denying that Horace is aware of incestuous feelings toward his stepdaughter, remarks: "Toward his sister Narcissa, however, he clearly does have them and may well be aware of them."[8] In the published text there is no evidence at all for such a statement. In the galleys, on the other hand, Horace's sexual attachment to both Narcissa and Little Belle was made amply clear, and to the extent that this part of his story is eliminated in revision, a whole dimension of irony is eliminated from the chronicle of Horace's confrontation with reality. In the original *Sanctuary* Faulkner developed the Horace-Narcissa relationship much more fully than he had done in *Sartoris*. For example, in a flashback to the time of Horace's courtship of Belle Mitchell, the following sequence is found in the galleys:

> "Dont talk to me about love," she said, her eyelids smoldering, lying in a wicker chair while Harry scuttled back and forth across the tennis court, applauding all shots in his harsh jarring voice; "you're in love with your sister. What do the books call it? What sort of complex?"
> "Not complex," he said. "Do you think that any relation with her could be complex?" A woman for whom even luck, life, simplified itself. Four months after his return from the war she married a man whom [*sic*] anyone could have known was doomed, who carried his fatality about with him, whom she had known all her life without having said four words to, or thought of half that many times save with serene and shocked distaste; three months after the wedding she was deserted; eight months later she became a mother and a widow.
> "Call it what you like," Belle said. "How did she come to let you go to the war, even with the Y.M.C.A.?"
> "I did the next best thing," he said. "I came back."
> "Yes," Belle said. "To her. Not to me."
> "Isn't one man at a time enough for you?"
> "Yes. And that wont be again, Horace. Do you hear? I dont need a lover. Even though it did take a war to show me that."
> "Did it last long enough to make you sure of that?"
> She looked at him, smoldering, contemplative, relaxed in the chair. "Your impossible hair," she said. She said: "So you hope one man is enough for her too, do you?" He said nothing. "That is, if you're the man, of course." She watched him from beneath her slow lids. "Horace, what are you going to do when she marries? What will you do the night a man makes—" He rose quickly, catching up his racket.
> "I think I'll play a set," he said. "Dont let that worry you. You know nothing about virginity. You've neither found it nor lost it."
> Two days before her wedding he said to her: "Is there any reason why you are marrying this particular blackguard?" She was reading in bed then; he had fetched her a letter which he had forgotten at noon. She lowered the book and looked at him, her brow beneath her loose hair broader than

[8]Cleanth Brooks, *William Faulkner: The Yoknapatawpha Country* (New Haven: Yale University Press, 1963), p. 129.

ever, with a serene placidity like that of heroic statuary. Suddenly he began to speak to her with thin fury, watching the sense of his words accomplish steadily behind her eyes, a half sentence behind, as though he were pouring them from a distance into a vessel. "What are you, anyway? What sort of life have you led for twenty-six years, that you can lie there with the supreme and placid stupidity of a cow being milked, when two nights from now—" he ceased. She watched him while the final word completed itself behind her eyes and faded. "Narcy," he said, "dont do it, Narcy. We both wont. I'll— Listen: we both wont. You haven't gone too far that you cant, and when I think what we . . . with this house, and all it— Dont you see we cant? It's not anything to give up: you dont know, but I do. Good God, when I think . . ."

She watched him while that sentence completed itself. Then she said: "You've got the smell of her all over you. Cant you tell it?"

After her marriage she moved out to the country, to her husband's. Horace did not attend the wedding; he merely saw her walk out of the house in a costume he had never seen before and would never see again; he never saw the two of them together after the wedding.

He saw her once before her husband died. He returned home at noon in the November rain and opened the door and they stood looking at one another.

"Narcy," he said, "has that blackguard—?"

"You fool! You fool! You haven't even an umbrella!" she said. (See Collation, p. 43)

Horace was here involved in a more complicated situation than is ever suggested in the published novel. Belle was sufficiently piqued by his fixation on his sister to retaliate by forcing him to contemplate a prospect he could not endure—that of Narcissa's giving herself to another man. Narcissa was sufficiently jealous of Belle ("You've got the smell of her all over you," she said in answer to Horace's plea) to strike back by planning to marry a man "whom she had known all her life without having said four words to, or thought of half that many times save with serene and shocked distaste." Horace, though powerfully attracted to Belle, was willing to give her up in order to keep his sister for himself; compared to his love for Narcissa, mere sex "is not anything to give up: you dont know, but I do." Confronted with her determination to marry Bayard Sartoris, he retaliated with a harsh epithet: "you can lie there with the supreme and placid stupidity of a cow being milked." (In the revised text the word *stupid* is never applied to Narcissa by Horace but is used descriptively by the omniscient author. See *Sanctuary*, pp. 25 and 102.)

Even Narcissa's marriage and motherhood had failed to break the bond that tied Horace to her in the original version. Ten years later, as we learn in another passage in the galleys, part of his motivation for leaving his wife was his belief "that the fact that he has quit one woman should enhance his value in the eyes of another—certainly in those of her enemy": that is, Narcissa (see Collation, p. 65). And after walking out on Belle he came back to Narcissa, whom he had not seen in six months or so, "with something of the chaotic emotions of a bridegroom of twenty-one" (see Collation, p. 63). Even this long after the death of Narcissa's husband, Horace's jealousy still interrupted his attempt to analyze his own relationship with his sister:

> He seemed to have expected her to be impervious not only to marriage, but to Sartorises as well. Yet even as the car entered the drive that led up to the square white house in its park of locusts and oaks, entering that atmosphere with which four generations of cold-blooded men clinging violently to their outworn traditions of human behavior had imbued the very soil on which they had lived, he was saying Damn that brute. Damn that brute. And later, pushing the mop back and forth with an awkward and ludicrous escapement of approximately enough energy to gin a bale of cotton, he thought of his sister as a figure enchanted out of all time between a bedridden old woman eighty-nine years old who summed in her person the ultimate frustration of all the furious folly of that race, and a nine-year-old boy emerging full-fledged from the soft haze of childhood into a tradition that had violently slain three men in four generations while in the throes of its own rigor-mortis. He had expected a woman to follow a man whom she had neither married nor borne, into that region of truth divorced from all reality which no woman is fool enough to assay; to follow the very man who had just repudiated that region of reality divorced from truth which women accept and make liveable. (See Collation, p. 82)

In the galleys Horace's incestuous attachment to Narcissa was traced back to his childhood, when he lost his mother. Several of the passages Faulkner eliminated in revision afford revealing glimpses of the mother-son relationship that preceded the brother-sister relationship:

> On the second night [after Horace's arrival at Narcissa's home] he dreamed that he was a boy again and waked himself crying in a paroxysm of homesickness like that of a child away from home at night, alone in a strange room. It seemed to him that not only the past two days, but the last thirty-five years had been a dream, and he waked himself calling his mother's name in a paroxism of terror and grief. [Several lines omitted]
> After a while he could not tell whether he were awake or not. He could still sense a faint motion of curtains in the dark window and the garden smells, but he was talking to his mother too, who had been dead thirty years. She had been an invalid, but now she was well; she seemed to emanate that abounding serenity as of earth which his sister had done since her marriage and the birth of her child. (See Collation, p. 83)

> It seemed to him that he came upon himself and his sister, upon their father and mother, who had been an invalid so long that the one picture of her he retained was two frail arms rising from a soft falling of lace, moving delicately to an interminable manipulation of colored silk, in fading familiar gestures in the instant between darkness and sunlight. (See Collation, p. 85)

> Once when he was a boy he had two possums in a barrel. A negro told him to put a cat in with them if he wanted to see something, and he had done

so. When he could move at all he ran to his mother in a passion of crying that sent him staggering and vomiting toward the house. All that night he lay beneath an ice-pack in a lighted room, tearing himself now and then by main strength out of writhing coil of cat entrails, toward the thin, shawled figure of his mother sitting beside the bed. (See Collation, p. 116)

From such passages it seems clear that Horace was an unusually sensitive boy whose dependence on his mother was increased by his awareness of her illness and the danger of losing her. This sense of a threat to his security, shortly confirmed by his mother's death, never left Horace. Thirty years later he woke from a nightmare, calling his mother's name in an agony of homesickness. It is notable, too, that after marrying Belle he went into debt to avoid selling his childhood home. His need to cling to the tranquil security of the past was suggested in another passage in the galleys:

In the center of the lawn, equidistant from either wing of the drive, between house and fence, was an oak. It was old and thick and squat, impenetrable to sun or rain. It was circled by a crude wooden bench, onto the planks of which the bole, like breasts of that pneumatic constancy so remote from lungs as to be untroubled by breath, had croached and over-bosomed until supporting trestles were no longer necessary. He sat on the bench, smoking, his back against the tree, remembering how on summer afternoons, all four of them would sit there while the spent summer rain murmured among the leaves and the thick breath of the honeysuckle bore up the slope in rich gusts, and usually a mockingbird somewhere in the peaceful twilight-colored rain already broken to the westward by a yellow wash of dying sunlight. (See Collation, p. 87)

The image of the overdeveloped breasts hinted at the connection in Horace's experience between security and sex. This connection went back to the period following his mother's death, when he apparently turned to his sister as a kind of mother-substitute. That he saw Narcissa in such a role was suggested by the statement that Horace, even as a middle-aged man, felt in her "that quality that seemed to take him by the shoulders as though he were a little boy and turn him about to face himself" (see Collation, p. 63). He also felt toward her as if they were lovers, so that it was a double-stranded bond with which young Horace attached himself to his sister.

Since his sexual feelings had to be repressed, the adult Horace finally turned for physical release to the provocative Belle Mitchell. The association in his mind of the two women was clear enough in the galleys. There was an explicit statement of his own thought as he left the Old Frenchmans place after drinking too much: "He tried to think of his sister, of Belle. But they seemed interchangeable now: two tiny, not distinguishable figures like two china figurines seen backward through a telescope" (see Collation, p. 53). Later, more suggestively, Horace "thought of Belle, then he was thinking of the three of them. He saw Belle and Narcissa and the woman with the child on her lap, all sitting on the cot in the jail'' (see Collation, p. 110). Ruby was an appropriate addition to the fused image because of Horace's response to her sexual attraction.

In the galleys Horace's substitution for his sister of a woman who served only a sexual need ended by tarnishing his marital relationship. Belle, he told himself after leaving her, "had chosen Kinston because of that land, the black, rich, foul, unchaste soil which seemed to engender money out of the very embrace of the air which lay flat upon it" (see Collation, p. 42). Moreover, on the afternoon he arrived at Narcissa's home "with something of the chaotic emotions of a bridegroom of twenty-one," he thought with retrospective distaste of "the tawdry shabbiness of that other [afternoon] where a marriage ceremony had neither promised nor meant any new emotional experience, since long before that hour Belle had taught him to believe that he was merely temporarily using Harry Mitchell's body, contriving somehow to dampen the rosy ardor of surreptitiousness with a quality turgid, conjugal and outworn; wearing her second husband like a lover, the lover like a garment whose sole charm for her lay in the belief that no other woman had one exactly like it; clinging to a certain emotional inviolation with a determination very like prurience turned upside down" (see Collation, p. 63). Thus, appropriately enough, Horace's temptation to leave his wife was turned into action by a soiled handkerchief untidily stuffed behind her dressing-table mirror.

As he himself was unconsciously aware, however, it was not the marital relationship that had defiled Horace. Since Belle was identified in his mind with Narcissa, who in turn was identified with his mother, he lay under the roof of the sister he had incestuously desired and, in a dream, blamed his mother for his twisted sexuality. Just after the nightmare about his boyhood, from which he woke "in a paroxysm of homesickness . . . calling his mother's name in a paroxysm of terror and grief," he had another dream, in which he fused his mother with his wife and with the woman he had met and desired at the Old Frenchmans place—an image of evil so horrifying that he associated it with the blackness he had smelled in Popeye:

[His mother] sat on the side of the bed, talking to him. With her hands, her touch, because he realised that she had not opened her mouth. Then he saw that she wore a shapeless garment of faded calico and that Belle's rich, full mouth burned suddenly out of the halflight, and he knew that she was about to open her mouth and he tried to scream at her, to clap his hand to her mouth. But it was too late. He saw her mouth open; a thick, black liquid welled in a bursting bubble that splayed out upon her fading chin and the sun was shining on his face and he was thinking He smells black. He smells like that black stuff that ran out of Bovary's mouth when they raised her head. (See Collation, p. 83)

16

Horace's confrontation with evil, as Faulkner originally wrote the story, brought him at last to the climactic discovery of his own evil. Long before he left his wife, who had proved to be such an inadequate substitute for his sister, he had turned yearningly to his stepdaughter. This situation is all but eliminated from the published novel, in which there are only four references to Little Belle: the scene of her dissimulation (*Sanctuary*, p. 13), Horace's later contemplation of the sin in her face (*Sanctuary*, p. 162), his association of her with the rape of Temple (*Sanctuary*, p. 215), and his telephone conversation with her after his return to his wife (*Sanctuary*, p. 293). Thus Edmond L. Volpe states categorically: "Benbow's relationship with his stepdaughter has drawn the attention of critics. A number have argued that Horace's attachment to the girl is rooted in sexual desire. It is not."[9] As we have seen, Cleanth Brooks agrees that there is no awareness of sexual feeling on Horace's part. In the galleys, however, the sexual element in Horace's attachment to Little Belle was repeatedly made clear, as the following passages will illustrate:

> Then she cried "No! No!" flinging herself upon him in a myriad secret softnesses beneath firm young flesh and thin small bones. "I didn't mean that. Horace! Horace!" (See Collation, p. 42)

> On the desk sat a photograph in a silver frame. Within the frame the small, soft face mused in sweet chiaroscuro. He looked at it quietly, wondering at what age a man ceases to believe he must support a certain figure before even the women at whose young intimacies he has made one: counsellor, hand-maiden, and friend. Upon the silence there seemed to lie the reverberant finality of the slammed door, and he thought of Little Belle beyond it, lying face-down on the bed probably, in that romantic despair, that dramatic self-pity of the young. . . . From the desk he took a pipe and tobacco pouch. Then he tried to slip the photograph inside his breast pocket, but the frame was too wide. He worked it free of the frame and it went in. (See Collation, p. 45)

> Then he would go to his room, where the suitcase stayed in the locked closet, where Little Belle's photograph was propped against a book on the table. He stood for a while before it, looking at the soft, sweet, vague face, thinking quietly how even at forty-three a man . . . that incomprehensible conviction of aging flesh that respect is due that commonest phenomenon in life: an accumulation of hours, breaths, temporarily in a single impermanent clot. Then he would go to bed, to lie in the darkness while the scents from the garden came up from below upon the soft, dark, blowing air, not thinking of anything at all. (See Collation, p. 82)

> "It's when I think of Little Belle; think that at any moment . . ." Against the book on the table the photograph sat under the lamp. Along the four edges of it was the narrow imprint of the missing frame. The face wore an expression of sweet and bemused self-consciousness. The short hair was

---

[9]Volpe, *Reader's Guide to Faulkner*, p. 143.

straight and smooth, neither light nor dark; the eyes darker than light and with a shining quality beneath soft and secret lids; a prim smooth mouth innocently travestied by the painted bow of the period. He began to whisper Damn him, damn him, tramping back and forth before the photograph. (See Collation, p. 99) [The "him" here seems to be Little Belle's potential seducer, about whom Horace felt just as he had felt earlier about Narcissa's husband. He had thought then: "Damn that brute. Damn that brute."]

Damn it, it is a civilised age, Horace thought, tramping back and forth while the sweet, soft, secret face came and went beneath the cylindrical blur of highlight which the lamp cast upon the glossy surface of the portrait, [*sic*] We are civilised, no matter how hard we try not to be. The stupidity of it, of believing that evil is merely an empty sound called daring; merely a closet of shiny costumes from which you can dress yourself for an evening. It's because they are fools enough to believe that older people, grown people, are wiser than they; because they believe that they must do all the things the magazines and movies tell them are expected of young people. Teaching them that the courageous thing is to live your own life, when nobody has an own life at sixty, let along sixteen. "Damn him, damn him," he whispered, tramping back and forth before the photograph.

If we'd just let them alone, he thought, thinking of the potential evil in everyone, even children; thinking of Temple back at school, spending perhaps one sleepless night in which for a little while and for the first time since she was born, she had completely forgot herself. Not over one night, he said. Then she'll realise that she has escaped and then it'll be a whispered tale over a box of candy, probably clumped pinpoints of cigarettes in the secure dark and soft gasps and crowded surges under fleeting silk, like puppies in a basket, five or six in the bed. But to think that by merely existing, drawing breath, they should be at the mercy of such . . ." "Damn him," he whispered, "damn him," tramping back and forth while the soft, bemused face blurred and faded in and out of the photograph. (See Collation, p. 101) [Here, just as the image of Belle merged with that of Narcissa in Horace's mind, the image of Temple Drake began to merge with that of Little Belle. In the revised version Faulkner left only one such identification, the significance of which is debatable, as will appear below.]

He discovered then that he had forgotten the book. The photograph was still propped against it—the very thing which had driven him from bed to walk four and three quarters miles in the darkness—and his inner eye showed it to him suddenly, blurred by the highlight, and beside it his freshly loaded pipe. (See Collation, p. 104) [Here again the two girls were associated in Horace's mind as he left for Oxford to look for Temple.]

When he [Clarence Snopes] had gone Horace entered the house and turned on the light, blinking after the subtle treachery of the moon. Little Belle's photograph sat on the mantel. He took it down, looking at it. The light hung on a shadeless cord, low; the shadow of his body lay upon the photograph. He moved it so that the light fell upon it, then drew it back into the shadow again. The difference was too intangible to discern, even by its own immediate comparison; the white still white, the black still black, the secret, musing expression unaltered. Delicate, evocative, strange, looking up out of the shadow with a crass brazenness, a crass belief that the beholder were blind. (See Collation, p. 109)

Perhaps Horace's repressed feeling about his stepdaughter was also clearly communicated in a passage revealing the sexual coloring of the impulse aroused in him by the young woman who, in the original version of the story, was several times identified with Little Belle: "He would sub-poena Temple; he thought in a paroxysm of raging pleasure of flinging her into the courtroom, of stripping her: This is what a man has killed another over. This, the offspring of respectable people: let them blush for shame, since he could never blush for anything again. Stripping her, background, environment, all" (see Collation, p. 110).

After so much emphasis on the nature of Horace's preoccupation with Little Belle, there seems no room for doubt, in the galleys, about what was happening in Horace's tortured vision of the rape of Temple:

> He found the light and turned it on. The photograph sat on the dresser. He took it up, holding it in his hands. Little Belle's face dreamed with that quality of sweet chiaroscuro. Communicated to the cardboard by some quality of the light or perhaps by some infinitesimal movement of his hands, his own breathing, the face appeared to breathe in his palms in a shallow bath of highlight, beneath the slow, smokelike tongues of invisible honeysuckle. Almost palpable enough to be seen, the scent filled the room and the small face seemed to swoon in a voluptuous languor, blurring still more, fading, leaving upon his eye a soft and fading aftermath of invitation and voluptuous promise and secret affirmation like a scent itself.
>
> Then he knew what that sensation in his stomach meant. He put the photograph down hurriedly and went to the bathroom. He opened the door running and fumbled at the light. But he had not time to find it and he gave over and plunged forward and struck the lavatory and leaned upon his braced arms while the shucks set up a terrific uproar beneath her thighs. Lying with her head lifted slightly, her chin depressed like a figure lifted down from a crucifix, she watched something black and furious go roaring out of her pale body. She was bound naked on her back on a flat car moving at speed through a black tunnel, the blackness streaming in rigid threads overhead, a roar of iron wheels in her ears. The car shot bodily from the tunnel in a long upward slant, the darkness overhead now shredded with parallel attenuations of living fire, toward a crescendo like a held breath, an interval in which she would swing faintly and lazily in nothingness filled with pale, myriad points of light. Far beneath her she could hear the faint, furious uproar of the shucks. (*Sanctuary*, p. 215)

The published book (in which the passage is unchanged from the original version but lacks the preparation which Faulkner initially made for it) allows a sharp difference of opinion about the significance of this episode, as has already been pointed out. Cleanth Brooks tries to clarify the passage: "In the last sentence Little Belle has not only been fused with Temple;

she has fused with Horace himself, who in an agony of empathy has felt himself into the raped girl's ordeal. This passage has been interpreted by several critics as a revelation to Horace of the evil within himself—incestuous feelings which he suddenly realizes he has for his stepdaughter. In Horace's unconscious mind there may indeed lurk such feelings, but I believe it would have required a psychiatrist to reveal them to Horace."[10] Horace's vision, as the story was originally written, involved more than empathy for the raped girl's ordeal, and Horace needed no psychiatrist to reveal the truth to him. Little Belle's teasing presence in his thoughts had been repeatedly revealed in the galleys. Now he was goaded beyond endurance by his lustful response to the "invitation and voluptuous promise and secret affirmation" which he sees in the face in the photograph. Horace was not visualizing a reported scene when the two figures in an alley-mouth appeared to him, "the man speaking in a low tone unprintable epithet after epithet in a caressing whisper, the woman motionless before him as though in a musing swoon of voluptuous ecstasy" (see *Sanctuary*, p. 214). Rather, this was his wishful image of himself, for he had already admitted his share in the guilt of Temple's lust: "Better for her if she were dead tonight, Horace thought, walking on. For me, too. . . . And I too; thinking how that were the only solution. Removed, cauterised out of the old and tragic flank of the world" (*Sanctuary*, p. 214). In short, in Horace's vision of the rape he had heard about, he himself became the ravisher of Little Belle. It was this realization which led to the image of the girl as his sacrificial victim: during her graphically described orgasm she lay "with her head lifted slightly, her chin depressed like a figure lifted down from a crucifix." And it was this realization, as it first dawned on him, that led to the death wish for both Temple and himself.

Though all this seems clear enough in the galleys, in the published text the passage is not entirely intelligible after all the deletions Faulkner made in his revision. At any rate, most commentators have not found in the passage Horace's confrontation of his own evil. Instead, *Sanctuary* is usually said to depict the debilitating results of Horace's realization, finally, that women are not by nature pure and innocent. Since Horace has long ago made such a discovery about Belle, however, and has made it again about Little Belle just before leaving his home, surely the revelation of Temple's corruption alone is not enough to precipitate the agonized nausea and the death wish he experiences after talking with her.

To the extent, then, that the revised novel comes out as an account of the belated disillusionment of a middle-aged adolescent, the original version was a much more credible story. Up to this point, that is. For there was a curious disappointment in store. Having set up the background for Horace's self-confrontation and then having vividly dramatized the experience itself, Faulkner neglected to follow through with a meaningful resolu-

---

[10]Brooks, *William Faulkner*, p. 129.

tion. In "The Dead," another story of self-confrontation, Joyce depicts the impact on Gabriel Conroy of a comparable moment: Conroy glimpses the resurrection that can follow the death of the ego. Faulkner, however, did not show us the result of Horace's discovery about himself. Or rather, he suggested that the presumably devastating experience had no effect at all. In the trial Horace gave up only when Temple perjured herself; there was no suggestion that he now felt unworthy to continue acting as the defender of right against wrong. And afterward he simply returned to Belle and picked up his life where he had left it. Even his comment on Little Belle, in a letter to Narcissa, was uncolored by any self-judgment:

> "Little Belle is not at home. Thank God: at what age does man cease to believe he must support a certain figure before his women-folks? She is at a house-party. Where, Belle did not say, other than it divulging to be in the exact center of bad telephone connections. Thank God she is no flesh and blood of mine. I thank God that no bone and flesh of mine has taken that form which, rife with its inherent folly, knells and bequeaths its own disaster, untouched. Untouched, mind you. That's what hurts. Not that there is evil in the world; evil belong [sic] in the world: it is the mortar in which the bricks are set. It's that they can be so impervious to the mire which they reveal and teach us to abhor; can wallow without tarnishment in the very stuff in the comparison with which their bright, tragic, fleeting magic lies. Cling to it. Not through fear; merely through some innate instinct of female economy, as they will employ any wiles whatever to haggle a butcher out of a penny. (See Collation, p. 117)

This wry observation about Little Belle's (and womankind's) affinity for evil seems incomprehensibly aloof after the catharsis of Horace's vision of the girl crucified by his lust. Moreover, surely Temple had not seemed to Horace, or to the reader, "untouched . . . impervious to the mire." Most incomprehensible of all is Horace's further revelation that he was merely settling back into his old relationship with his stepdaughter. In his telephone conversation with her he revealed both his claim upon her attention and his jealousy of her young suitor:

> Thank God I have not and will never have a child—and for that reason I have assailed not only a long distance, but a rural, line at eleven P.M. in order to hear a cool, polite, faintly surprised young voice on an unsatisfactory wire; a voice that, between polite inanities in response to inanities, carried on a verbal skirmishing with another one—not feminine—without even doing me the compliment of trying to conceal the fact that she had been squired to the telephone; needs must project over the dead wire to me, whose hair she has watched thinning for ten years, that young mammalian rifeness which she discovered herself less long ago than I the fact that, [sic] to anyone less than twenty-five years old, I am worse than dead. (See Collation, p. 117)

In his letter to Narcissa, then, the sensitive, idealistic Horace seemed totally out of character: he was able to forget, or at least to ignore successfully, his tortured discovery of the sexual desire he had felt for Little Belle. In other words, Faulkner made only a careless gesture at tying up the ends of the story he had undertaken—the story of a man who, idealistically trying to right a wrong committed by another, discovered a comparable wrong within himself. Horace used Narcissa, Belle, and Little Belle as outlets for his unacknowledged sexuality, and even his offer to defend Goodwin free of charge was partly motivated by the physical attraction of Ruby. Up to the point of Horace's self-discovery, the original version of *Sanctuary* was convincing and compelling in spite of many evidences of hasty work. Unaccountably, however, Faulkner seems not to have thought through the final question: how did Horace deal with his new self-knowledge?

Instead of coming to grips with this problem in his revision, Faulkner chose an easier course. He altered his conception of his protagonist to suit the ending he had already written. By simply cutting out the passages that revealed the character's sexual problems and thus his hidden capacity for evil, he turned Horace into a genuinely well-intentioned man whose problem is his innocence—an innocence so impenetrable that only in middle age is he forced at last to acknowledge that women are innately no purer than men. This discovery is so demoralizing that, after his dazed surrender in court, he can only fall back on what Lawrance Thompson calls a self-excusing rationalization: "Eventually Horace seeks that familiar sanctuary of insisting that he is in no way to blame for what happens, because the forces of evil are so highly organized and powerful that they have reduced the forces of good to impotence."[11]

Having eliminated the labyrinthine probing back into the past that had made Horace the complex and credible character he was, Faulkner apparently tried to make up for the loss by downgrading him to the role of co-protagonist with Temple and by streamlining the story for theatrical impact. Appropriately he supplied what Linton Massey calls the "smash finish" of the lynching scene. Like the hanging of Popeye, which occurs in both versions, the lynching of Goodwin is an ironic comment on the workings of justice as administered by men like Horace, but it functions in no other way. Horace is not shown to be affected by what he witnesses. The episode serves only to highlight an effect that is already clear; it is a good stage device and little more.

Also added in revision, the next chapter with its detailed account of Horace's return to Belle is, of course, more dramatically effective than the bare summary in Horace's letter to Narcissa. Even so, Faulkner leaves a loose end that is vaguely irritating. Horace repeatedly tries to say to Little Belle something that he never finishes:

> "Yes?" her voice came back thin and faint. "What is it? Is anything wrong?"
>
> "No, no," Horace said. "I just wanted to tell you hello and good night."

[11]Thompson, *William Faulkner,* p. 108.

"Tell what? What is it? Who is speaking?" Horace held the receiver, sitting in the dark hall.

"It's me, Horace. Horace. I just wanted to—"

Over the thin wire there came a scuffling sound; he could hear Little Belle breathe. Then a voice said, a masculine voice: "Hello, Horace; I want you to meet a—"

"Hush!" Little Belle's voice said, thin and faint; again Horace heard them scuffling; a breathless interval. "Stop it!" Little Belle's voice said. "It's Horace! I live with him!" Horace held the receiver to his ear. Little Belle's voice was breathless, controlled, cool, discreet, detached. "Hello. Horace. Is Mamma all right?"

"Yes. We're all right. I just wanted to tell you . . ."

"Oh. Good night."

"Good night. Are you having a good time?"

"Yes. Yes. I'll write tomorrow. Didn't Mamma get my letter today?"

"I dont know. I just—"

"Maybe I forgot to mail it. I wont forget tomorrow, though. I'll write tomorrow. Was that all you wanted?"

"Yes. Just wanted to tell you . . ." (*Sanctuary*, p. 293)

What does Horace want to tell Little Belle? With his wife overhearing the conversation, it can hardly be anything private and important. Moreover, in the published novel Horace is never clearly shown to have sexual feelings for his stepdaughter, so why has he telephoned at all? In the galleys the call was presumably motivated by the same incestuous desire he had felt from the beginning, but Faulkner's revision of the passage arouses the reader's curiosity for no good reason.

The most notable change at the end of the book is the addition of the long passage detailing Popeye's birth and childhood (see Collation, p. 119). Structurally, the information is awkwardly tacked on, like the afterthought it is. Thematically, the reversal of attitude toward Popeye is also disturbing. Instead of viewing him with horror, as we have done until this point in the story, we now realize that he is not simply an evil man but a pitiable victim of heredity and environment. This introduction of a deterministic view of Popeye suggests the possibility of such a view of several other characters who are judged harshly in the novel, notably Temple, Narcissa, and Horace. It seems particularly inconsistent for Faulkner to have added Popeye's extenuating background after removing nearly all the background he had originally supplied for Horace—a background that might have led to a charitable view of the man instead of the vague dissatisfaction or even impatience felt by some readers of the published novel.

The portrayal of Popeye seemed more effective in the original version, in which he was depicted as an incarnation of evil, comparable to Shakespeare's Iago. Moreover, in the galleys there were several vivid touches that Faulkner omitted in revision. Horace, after the evening he had spent at the Old Frenchmans place, remembered Popeye as "the slim black one without any chin, with his quarulous [sic] adolescent's voice, who didn't even drink because he said it made him sick to his stomach like a dog and who was always trying to get someone to light a lantern and go some where with him" (see Collation, p. 71). This quality of adolescent peevishness—which makes Graham Greene's perhaps derivative character, Pinky, so believable in *Brighton Rock*—was further developed in another passage, where the profane tough guy revealed the insecurity of a child:

> Then he returned to the porch and tried again to persuade the halfwit to get the lantern and take him somewhere and the halfwit refused, and the thug stood there and cursed him in a cold, savage voice and the halfwit guffawed and Horace could hear his bare feet scuffing slowly on the boards. The thug lit a cigarette, his face coming out of the match, and his hooked little nose and no chin and his slanted hat which he had not even removed at supper, and he leaned against the wall for a while, listening to the talk with a kind of savage moroseness. Sulking, like a child that's mad and stays around to show it's mad. There was something childlike about him: his slenderness, smallness; an air of petulant bewilderment. (See Collation, p. 73)

Two of Popeye's possessions, all description of which is omitted in the revised novel, added credibility to the character as originally conceived. First, there was his car, "a long, thick, squatting car without a top; the kind you look at with a sort of respectful awe, like one of those shells that shoot once and cost two thousand dollars" (see Collation, p. 76). More particularly, there were his watches: "his dollar watch loose in his pocket like a coin, with the platinum chain across his vest and a turnip-shaped silver watch which wouldn't run on the end of it, which he had inherited from his grandfather, with a lock of his mother's hair in the back of the case. He showed the watch to Horace at the spring, before they came to the house" (see Collation, p. 74). With his childish insecurity and petulance, his ostentation that reminds one of another bootlegger named Jay Gatsby, and his sentimentality of the kind often found associated with brutality, the original Popeye was more alive than the revised character. According to Linton Massey, the flattening of Popeye's character heightens the effect of the novel. Faulkner's decision that "Popeye must be denied any such sentimental affectation as the ownership of a watch that belonged to his grandfather and had a lock of his mother's hair in the case," we are told, is in line with the elimination of "the domesticity and warmth of Miss Jenny, and the ascription of any humanity whatever to most of the characters."[12] This comment is echoed in Cleanth Brooks's discussion of some of the details that "rob Popeye of substance and make him a sinister black silhouette against the spring landscape."[13] If Faulkner's purpose in his revision was to make sure Popeye became too inhuman to warrant

---

[12] Massey, "Notes on the Unrevised Galleys," p. 204.

[13] Brooks, *William Faulkner*, p. 120.

any sympathy, he defeated his purpose by adding an account of the pitiably blighted childhood that produced the sinister figure.

The elimination not only of the warmth and domesticity of Miss Jenny, but also of the whole background of the Sartoris family, is a questionable change too. Most noteworthy among the omissions is the following passage:

Miss Jenny still had a fire in the evenings. The chair faced it. Beside the chair Saddie sat on the footstool. The boy leaned against the mantel, his face bold in the firelight, a little sullen.

On the wall beside the bed, where one lying in the bed could look at them by turning the head, were a number of portraits arranged in a certain order. The first was a faded tintype in an oval frame. A bearded face stared haughtily across the neck-cloth of the '50's, buttoned into a frock coat. The man was in the full flush of maturity's early summer; the whiskers virile, the nose high-bridged, the eyes quick-tempered and overbearing, and turning his head Horace saw a delicate replica of it above Miss Jenny's shawl, beneath the silver coronet of her hair, serenely profiled by the fire, and a shadowy, faintly sullen promise of it leaning against the mantel. He looked at the portrait again. Beside it hung a second and more hasty one, made in the field: the same man in a long gray tunic with the awry shoulder-straps of a Confederate colonel. His trousers were thrust into dusty boots, his gauntleted hands rested upon the hilt of a sabre, the bearded face shadowed by a broken plume.

"What are you doing?" Miss Jenny said. "Looking at the Rogues' Gallery?"

The boy said moodily: "Gowan said he'd take me, but she wouldn't let me go."

"Why, you wouldn't leave your mother and me alone, without a man in the house, would you?" Miss Jenny said.

"Horace is here," the boy said. "Who stayed with you before I was born?"

Next was a conventional photograph dated fifteen years ago. The man was about sixty, going bald, the mouth shaded by a thick moustache, the chin clean-shaven, a little heavy. The quick temper was there too, but blurred, as though by a film, a bafflement, something.

The next was also light-stained, faintly archaic. The face was thin, dark, with dark hair above a high brow. The face above the broad collar, the puffed cravat and the high lapels of the early 1900's was that of a sick man. It was clean-shaven, haughty, young and proud.

Next was a photograph of two boys with long curls, in identical velvet suits. They were not long definitely out of babyhood, yet there was already upon the infantile chubbiness of their faces a shadow as though from the propinquity of the faces above them; a quality that utterly relegated the curls and the velvet, and already there was a distinction between them, although they were obviously twins.

The next three were in a row. The middle one was a painted miniature, the face that of a boy of seven or so.

At the fire Miss Jenny spoke. She had not moved. Her head lay back, her hands on the arms of the chair, the firelight rosy upon her. "Saddie. What are you doing?"

"Aint doin nothin, Miss Jenny."

"What does the devil find for idle hands?"

"Mischuf, Miss Jenny."

"Then what are you going to do about it?"

Horace watched Saddie go to the table and lift down a sewing basket. Squatting on the floor above it she delved into it with that intense gravity of a monkey or a coon. She replaced it and returned to the stool with a piece of coarse needlework and a dependent needle, and sat again and began to ply the needle by firelight, her head bent, tongue in cheek, her still-babyish hands moving like ink upon the white cloth, with the terrific awkwardness of a monkey or a coon.

"Yes, sir," Miss Jenny said, "I cant have any idle folks around me. If you want to be a house-nigger, that is. Or maybe you dont? maybe you want to be a field-hand and wear shoes and stockings only on Sunday?"

Saddie giggled. Bent over the work, she continued to chuckle. "Nome, Miss Jenny," she said, her voice going on in rich, dying chuckles, as though of its own accord.

"She oughtn't to try to sew in that light," Horace said. "I can hardly see her hands on the cloth, even."

"Fiddlesticks. They're part owl, anyway. Aint you, gal?"

Saddie chuckled, without looking up. "Nome, Miss Jenny. I aint no owl."

"What are you then?" Saddie bent over her slow, terrific hands, the cap crisp upon her neat pigtails. "Who made you, then?" Miss Jenny said.

"God made me. Ise a child of God." She said it in a fainting, rapturous voice; immediately she was about to chuckle again.

"You, nigger gal! Why did He make you?" Saddie hung her head above her unceasing hands. "You, nigger! Talk out!"

"For His greater glory," Saddie said.

"And who are you after that?"

"Ise a Sarto'is han'-maiden."

"Why couldn't you say so, then?" Miss Jenny turned and looked at Horace's back. "What do you think of that?"

"Habet, O most eminent republican," he said. He was looking at the miniature. The curls were still there, the eyes bold and merry, the mouth sweet. It was flanked on one side by a hasty snapshot. Both operator and subject appeared to have been moving when the camera was snapped, for the picture was both lop-sided and blurred as well as out of focus. The subject's head emerged from an elliptical manhole in a tubular affair on the side of which the effigy of a rabbit projected its painted ears into the picture. To the front arc of the pit a narrow screen curved tightly, and two struts slanted upward into a flat surface at right angles in horizontal perspective, from which the pistol-grip of a machine gun tilted. The face, beneath a wild thatch, was in the act of turning when the camera snapped. It was full of movement, travesties [*sic*] by the dead celluloid, the eyes squinted and the mouth open, as though he were either shouting or laughing.

On the other side of the miniature was another conventional photograph. In uniform, with orderly hair, he lounged in a deep chair placed cleverly to bring the subdued light onto his bleak, humorless face, and again Horace looked toward the fire, at the boy leaning there, at the brooding face, the mouth emerging sullenly from childhood, then back to the bleak eyes and the sullen mouth in the photograph.

"Did you see the last one?" Miss Jenny said. "Gowan snapped it."

"He went to Virginia, too," the boy said. "But he wasn't an aviator like my father was."

The next row consisted of nine photograps [sic] of the boy, one for each of his years, ranging from that in which he sprawled naked on a fur rug, through his various avatars in rompers, velvet; as an Indian, a cowboy, a soldier, a groomsman in a diminutive tailcoat, to the final one in which he sat the pony, erect, hand on hip, a salvaged revolver-frame in his waistband, a small negro perched like a monkey on the withers of a gaunt mule in the background. This was Sundy, Saddie's twin; Saturday and Sunday. Horace had named them: two minute creatures with still, shiny eyes like four shoe-buttons, born to Elnora the cook, a tall woman in middle life who was unmarried at the time.

Narcissa entered, with a newspaper. She drew a chair up and opened the paper and began to read aloud, lurid accounts of arson and adultery and homicide, in her grave contralto voice. Miss Jenny listened, her head lying back and her eyes closed, her thin profile rosy and serene in the firelight. Her husband had been killed in 1862, on the second anniversary of her wedding-day. She had not spoken his name in sixty-seven years. (See Collation, p. 65)

Since this family history was a recapitulation from the novel *Sartoris*, perhaps it gave the original version of *Sanctuary* a certain "warmed-over flavor," as Mr. Massey puts it.[14] Undeniably, too, the use of a series of photographs was a static, undramatic device for conveying background information. And Saddie (let alone Sundy) served no more purpose here than she did in an earlier appearance (see Collation, p. 60, and compare Horace's equally useless account of Bory and Sundy on p. 58). Nevertheless, Horace's interest in these matters did help to develop a side of his personality barely suggested in the published novel—his need for the rooted stability represented by the Sartoris tradition and Miss Jenny's sturdiness of character. It was his loss of such stability, as has been suggested, that led to the incestuous bond with Narcissa and made him unwilling to sell the unused family home.

Several other matters deserve attention. No purpose at all was served by the reminder in the galleys of the Byron Snopes episode in *Sartoris*:

During the year before his sister's marriage she had received a series of anonymous love-letters written by a scarce literate man. Inarticulate, obscene and sincere, she read them with detached equanimity, seeming to

[14]Massey, "Notes on the Unrevised Galleys," p. 204.

have no curiosity whatever regarding the author, not even bothering to destroy them. One night they were stolen: that was the only time Horace ever saw her lose her poise. He saw her then in the throes of a passion nearer maternal than actual motherhood ever roused; not with outrage or fear, but at the idea of having letters addressed to her read by someone she did not know. (See Collation, p. 91)

In this passage Faulkner removed the element that gives the episode point in *Sartoris*: Narcissa's deliberate preservation of the letters because she secretly craves the very kind of dirt that, in her role as the unravished bride of Horace's idealization, she scorns in Belle. The passage revealed not Narcissa's hypocrisy but her passion for privacy, a quality of no thematic relevance in the story.

Another minor omission, on the other hand, seems a loss. Instead of describing Lee Goodwin merely as a man with "a lean, weathered face, the jaws covered by a black stubble; his hair was gray at the temples" (*Sanctuary*, p. 11), Faulkner originally presented the man in such a way as to convey an evaluation and make understandable his hold on Ruby. For example: "Goodwin sat so still in his tilted chair that after a while his immobility acquired a sort of personality. If Horace had not seen him by the lamp on the supper-table he could have told exactly how he looked, even to his brown eyes and his black head. He looked like a centurion in overalls and a blue shirt, Horace thought; like the sort of centurion who would have had a shot at the purple and made it go" (see Collation, p. 78).

Among many such minor revisions, one other particularly catches the eye. Faulkner apparently felt that Clarence Snopes's remark about the ten dollars given him by the Jew lawyer needed clarification. In the following passage the italicized portion is not found in the galleys:

When a jew lawyer can hold up an American, a white man, and not give him but ten dollars for something that two Americans, Americans, *southron gentlemen; a judge living in the capital of the State of Mississippi and a lawyer that's going to be as big a man as his paw some day, and a judge too;* when they give him ten times as much for the same thing than the lowlife jew, we need a law. I been a liberal spender all my life; whatever I had has always been my friends' too. But when a durn, stinking, lowlife *jew will refuse to pay an American one tenth of what another American, and a judge at that—*" (See Collation, p. 113)

The added information makes it perfectly clear that the two Americans who each gave Snopes a hundred dollars for his information about Temple are Judge Drake and Horace Benbow. It is still far from clear, though, why and by whom Snopes was beaten up, and why he was paid even ten dollars in addition to the beating.

A change of a different kind introduced confusion where none had existed before. The problem requiring attention arose when Faulkner eliminated the opening flashbacks and reorganized Horace's story in chronological sequence. Before shifting to the account of Temple at the Old Frenchmans place (Chapters IV-XIV), he had to get Horace to Narcissa's home and introduce the reader to Gowan Stevens. In his revision, therefore, Faulkner added a transitional paragraph at the beginning of Chapter III: "On the next afternoon Benbow was at his sister's home. It was in the country, four miles from Jefferson; the home of her husband's people. She was a widow, with a boy ten years old, living in a big house with her son and the great aunt of her husband: a woman of ninety, who lived in a wheel chair, who was known as Miss Jenny. She and Benbow were at the window, watching his sister and a young man walking in the garden. His sister had been a widow for ten years" (see Collation, p. 57). Later, picking up Horace's story after devoting eleven chapters to Temple, Faulkner forgot that he had already brought Horace to Narcissa's home, for Chapter XV begins thus: "Benbow reached his sister's home in the middle of the afternoon. It was four miles from town, Jefferson. He and his sister were born in Jefferson, seven years apart, in a house which they still owned, though his sister had wanted to sell the house when Benbow married the divorced wife of a man named Mitchell and moved to Kinston. Benbow would not agree to sell, though he had built a new bungalow in Kinston on borrowed money upon which he was still paying interest" (see Collation, p. 84).

On a first reading at least, one is momentarily uncertain whether the arrival described in Chapter XV is the same as that in Chapter III. In the earlier scene one assumes that Horace has arrived during or just before the visit of Gowan Stevens, which occurs shortly before suppertime. In the later scene, however, Horace arrives in the middle of the afternoon and has a talk with Narcissa about having left Belle; then, without any mention of Stevens's visit, we are told in a paragraph added in revision: "He stayed at his sister's two days. She had never been given to talking, living a life of serene vegetation like perpetual corn or wheat in a sheltered garden instead of a field, and during those two days she came and went about the house with an air of tranquil and faintly ludicrous tragic disapproval" (see Collation, p. 64). Of course, the fact that Horace has just left Belle makes it clear, upon reflection, that his talk with Narcissa in Chapter XV has to occur on the same afternoon as Stevens's visit in Chapter III, but the arrangement is an awkward one. It not only violates the chronological presentation in the revised novel; it also results in the confusing duplication of information about Narcissa's home.

These, then, are the most notable changes made in the revision of *Sanctuary*. They are not nearly so radical as Faulkner's later statements would indicate, nor does a comparison of the two versions bear out his description of the original novel as a "cheap" or "shabby" thing he "rewrote" so as not to shame his two preceding books. Actually, a better verb would be "rearranged," since the revision turns out to consist most strikingly of omissions and of changes in the order of presenting events—in other words, an alteration of the narrative method. This is an interesting fact when one looks forward and backward in the work of Faulkner, for *Sanctuary* was a turning point in his experimentation. In his next book, *Light in August,* he again employed a relatively straightforward method, closer to that of the revised *Sanctuary* than to that of the two preceding books. Then, as if unwilling to abandon an experiment that had not worked out to suit him the first time, he returned in *Absalom, Absalom!* to a narrative method comparable in some ways to that of the original *Sanctuary.*

Both *The Sound and the Fury* and *As I Lay Dying* are, in one sense, simple in design. As far as the angle of narration is concerned, both stories are like a structure composed exclusively of blocks laid one upon another. Each section or chapter is presented from a single point of view (that of a character or, in the final section of *The Sound and the Fury,* that of the omniscient author). In neither the felt presence of the organizing author nor the continued use of a single character as a central intelligence is there an inner framework to control the shape of the structure. By comparison, the use of point of view in the original *Sanctuary* and in *Absalom, Absalom!* is more complex, suggesting not building blocks but an elaborate design composed of many tiny fragments. In other words, a mosaic—or rather, if such a thing can be visualized, one transparent mosaic superimposed on and supplementing the design of another. That is, in both novels there is a story-within-a-story (Temple's within Horace's, Sutpen's within Quentin's), and it is the effect of the inner character upon the outer one that constitutes the main plot line. Both novels are explicitly organized by, and in part told by, the omniscient author, who nevertheless focuses the narration as a whole through the point of view of the central outer character. But only the action as a whole. In any scene of the story-within-a-story in the original *Sanctuary,* the point of view can shift to that of any character who may be involved, and a slightly different but comparable effect is achieved in *Absalom, Absalom!*

For example, in the original *Sanctuary* the author first set up the scene of Ruby telling Horace about the night Temple and Gowan spent at the Old Frenchmans place (or rather, Horace's remembrance of the scene, since it was a flashback from the present time of the novel): "She stood beside the bed, looking down at the child. 'There was a woman there,' she said. 'A young girl.' 'A—' Horace said. 'Oh,' he said. 'Yes. You'd better tell me about it'" (see Collation, p. 94, and *Sanctuary,* p. 131). Instead of continuing with Ruby's narrative, however, Faulkner shifted to an omniscient account of the background of Temple's date with Gowan: "Townspeople taking after-supper drives through the college grounds or an oblivious and bemused faculty member or a candidate for a master's degree on his way to the library would see Temple, a snatched coat under her arm and her long legs blonde with running, in speeding silhouette against the lighted windows of the Coop, as the women's dormitory was known, vanishing into the shadow beside the library wall, and perhaps a final squatting swirl of knickers or whatnot as she sprang into the car waiting there with engine running on that particular night" (see Collation, p. 94: Galley, ch. VII).

This direct dramatization continued to the point of Temple's entrance into Goodwin's dining room to face the frightening group of men, when the narrative shifted back to Horace and Ruby in the hotel room, and Ruby's account continued: "Tm he [*sic*] woman leaned above the child, her face bent toward it in a musing attitude, as though she were not seeing it. It lay beneath the faded, clean blanket, its hands upflung beside its head, as though it had died in the presence of an unbearable agony which had not had time to touch it. . . . 'Nobody wanted her out there. Lee has told them and told them they must not bring women out there, and I told her before it got dark they were not her kind of people and to get away from there' " (see Collation, p. 94). At the point in the story when Ruby told of leading Temple out to the barn, the narration shifted again to a direct dramatization, focused mainly through Temple's point of view:

> On their bare feet they moved like ghosts. They left the house and crossed the porch and went on toward the barn. When they were about fifty yards from the house the woman stopped and turned and jerked Temple up to her, and gripping her by the shoulders, their faces close together, she cursed Temple in a whisper, a sound no louder than a sigh and filled with fury . . .
> Temple waked lying in a tight ball, with narrow bars of sunlight falling across her face like the tines of a golden fork, and while the stiffened blood trickled and tingled through her cramped muscles she lay gazing quietly up at the ceiling. (See Collation, p. 96; Galley, ch. X, 154 ff.)

This dramatization was not interrupted again until Ruby took over the description of Temple's departure with Popeye:

> "But that girl," Horace said. "You know she was all right. You know that."
> The woman sat on the edge of the bed, looking down at the child. Motionless, her head bent and her hands still in her lap, she had that spent immobility of a chimney rising above the ruin of a house in the aftermath of a cyclone. "The car passed me about halfway back to the house," she said in a flat, toneless voice. "She was in it. I dont know what time it was. It was about half way back to the house."
> "You had turned around and were going back?"
> "I forgot to bring his bottle," she said. (See Collation, p. 97)

Such shifting of the angle of narration not only afforded perspectives from within and from without (the sensations of Temple versus the comments of Ruby). On a second level it also kept before us the impact of Ruby's narrative upon Horace. For example, the account of what happened after Popeye carried Temple away was interrupted by a shift to Horace's later remembrance of what he had heard, a reverie which, as noted above, revealed his association of Temple with Little Belle:

"It's when I think of Little Belle; think that at any moment . . ." Against the book on the table the photograph sat under the lamp. Along the four edges of it was the narrow imprint of the missing frame. The face wore an expression of sweet and bemused self-consciousness. The short hair was straight and smooth, neither light nor dark; the eyes darker than light and with a shining quality beneath soft and secret lids; a prim smooth mouth innocently travestied by the painted bow of the period. He began to whisper Damn him, damn him, tramping back and forth before the photograph . . . (See Collation, p. 99)

Finally, on a third level, the shifting angle of narration allowed Faulkner to hold Horace far enough away to afford a detached view of the intricate interplay. This was accomplished by the occasional interjection of authorial evaluations like the wry comment that Horace "moved about the tight and inscrutable desolation in a prolonged orgasm of sentimental loneliness" (see Collation, p. 85), or like the explanation that he hesitated to use Miss Jenny's telephone to check on Little Belle, "telling himself that the reason was that he did not want to disturb her, knowing that the reason was that he did not want even Miss Jenny to know what an old woman he was. But the real reason was that he was afraid to face in the darkness what he might find at the other end of the wire" (see Collation, p. 103).

In a comparable use of point of view in *Absalom, Absalom!* the omniscient author places Quentin at a distance by commenting, for example, that he "was still too young to deserve yet to be a ghost, but nevertheless having to be one for all that," (p. 9),[15] or by explaining that Quentin narrates to Shreve "with that overtone of sullen bemusement, of smouldering outrage" (p. 218). In one typical episode the author sets the scene of Quentin and Shreve talking in a room so cold that it is tomblike: "Yet they remained in it, though not thirty feet away was bed and warmth. . . . They both bore it as though in deliberate flagellant exaltation of physical misery transmogrified into the spirits' travail of the two young men during that time fifty years ago" (p. 345). We are then shifted to the point of view of Quentin, who, while listening to Shreve's recapitulation, withdraws so completely into his own visualization of a dramatic scene in 1864 that he relives Henry Sutpen's experience and shares Henry's point of view. In this way the scene simultaneously recreates a long-past event from its own perspective and dramatizes Quentin's consuming obsession with the old story, while the the comments of the author detach us enough so that we can appraise the interaction of the two stories with compassionate understanding.

The original *Sanctuary* is thus, in several ways, a highly interesting book. The "horrific" adventures of Temple may indeed have been conceived with an eye on the popular market, but in the novel that is preserved in the galleys Faulkner invested so much thought and artistry that one's final reaction is to repeat in bewilderment the question that has already been

---

[15]*Absalom, Absalom!*, Modern Library edition, 1951.

asked: why was the writer unwilling or unable to complete Horace's story meaningfully? In the first version he settled negligently for an ending that was out of character for Horace. In the revised version he obviated the difficulty by simplifying his portrayal of Horace to fit the ending for which he apparently could find no alternative. But the problem Faulkner put aside in 1931 demanded his attention at last. In *Requiem for a Nun*, returning to the question that seems to have eluded him twenty years before, he explores the repercussions of a person's discovery of his own evil. Only this time the self-confrontation is Temple's, not Horace's. All things considered, it looks as if in writing and revising *Sanctuary* Faulkner tried twice to clarify his conception of the Horace Benbow he had created in *Sartoris*, and felt he had failed both times, for he never used him as a character again. Instead, as early as 1931 in the story "Hair," he created Gavin Stevens to fill the kind of roles for which Horace might seem to have been the logical candidate.

Reference Chart

GALLEY

BOOK

GALLEY	BOOK
Chap. I, lines 1–7 (some cancellation)	Chap. XVI, page 110, lines 1–2
I, 7–43	XVI, 110, 2 —— 111, 15 (unchanged)
I, 44–54 (some cancellation)	XVI, 111, 15 —— 112, 3 (some addition) .
I, 55–60	XVI, 112, 3–7 (unchanged)
	XVI, 112, 7–8 (new)
I, 60–68	XVI, 112, 8–16 (unchanged)
I, 68–70 (some cancellation)	XVI, 112, 16
I, 70–73	XVI, 112, 16–18 (unchanged)
I, 73–87 (some cancellation)	XVI, 112, 18–30
I, 88–109	XVI, 112, 31 —— 113, 18 (unchanged)
I, 109–121 (some cancellation)	XVI, 113, 18
I, 122–169	XVI, 113, 18 —— 114, 30 (unchanged)
I, 169–182 (some cancellation)	XVI, 114, 30 —— 115, 3
I, 182–406	XVI, 115, 3 —— end of chapter (unchanged)
II, 1–242 (some cancellation)	II, 12, 24 —— 16, 8 (some addition)
II, 243–295 (canceled)	
II, 296–487 (some cancellation)	I, 3, 1 —— 7, 27 (some addition)
II, 488–495 (canceled)	
II, 496–638 (some cancellation)	II, 18, 24 —— end of chapter (some addition:
II, 639–675 (canceled)	see below, opposite Galley IV, 255–269)
III, 1–70 (canceled)	
III, 71–107 (some cancellation)	III, 23, 1–9; 23, 13 —— 24, 2 (some addition);
	26, 17–27
III, 108–140 (canceled)	
III, 141–146 (some cancellation)	III, 23, 10–12
III, 147–155 (canceled)	
III, 156–169 (some cancellation)	III, 24, 3–10 (some addition)
III, 169–303 (some cancellation)	III, 24, 11 —— 26, 16
III, 304–321 (canceled)	
III, 322–335 (some cancellation)	XV, 102, 10 —— 103, 15 (some addition)
III, 336–347 (canceled)	
III, 348–377 (some cancellation)	III, 26, 27 —— 27, 6
III, 378–589 (canceled)	
III, 590–642	XV, 103, 16 —— 105, 30 (some addition)

NOTE: This list of correspondences, though originally based on the valuable charts accompanying Linton Massey's article cited in the Introduction, differs from them in a number of ways.

GALLEY	BOOK
IV, 1–157 (canceled)	
IV, 158–219 (some cancellation)	I, 7, 28 — 8, 20; 8, 21 — end of chapter (new)
IV, 220–254 (canceled)	
IV, 255–269	II, 19, 12–28
IV, 270–294	II, 11, 1–14 (new); 11, 15 — 12, 23
IV, 295–352 (canceled)	
IV, 352–432 (some cancellation)	II, 16, 9–20 (new); 16, 21 — 18, 23
V, 1	XV, 103, 10 (unchanged)
V, 2–146 (canceled)	XV, 103, 10–15 (new); also see above, opposite Galley III, 322–335
V, 147–152 (some cancellation)	XV, 102, 1–9 (some addition)
V, 152–235 (canceled)	
V, 236–247 (some cancellation)	XV, 106, 1–18 (some addition)
V, 247–292 (canceled)	
V, 293–297	XV, 106, 18–23 (some addition)
V, 298–355 (canceled)	
V, 356–372	XV, 106, 24 — 107, 8 (unchanged)
V, 373–407 (canceled)	
V, 407–475	XV, 107, 8 — end of chapter (unchanged)
VI, 1–23	XVII, 122, 1 — 123, 2 (unchanged)
VI, 24–28 (canceled)	
VI, 29–32	XVII, 123, 3–9 (some addition)
VI, 33–67 (some cancellation)	XVII, 123, 10 — 124, 4
VI, 68–164	XVII, 124, 5 — 126, 23 (unchanged)
	XVII, 126, 24–25 (new)
VI, 165–179	XVII, 126, 26 — 127, 7 (unchanged)
VI, 180–198 (canceled)	XVII, 127, 8–17 (new)
VI, 199–298	XVII, 127, 17 — 130, 8 (unchanged)
VI, 299–314 (canceled)	XVII, 130, 9–14 (new)
VI, 315–317	XVII, 130, 14–16 (unchanged)
VI, 318–321 (canceled)	
VI, 321–354 (some cancellation)	XVII, 130, 17 — 131, 2 (some addition)
VI, 355–372	XVII, 131, 3 — end of chapter (unchanged)
VII, 1–397	IV, 28, 1 — end of chapter (unchanged)
VIII, 1–126	V, 39, 1 — end of chapter (unchanged)
VIII, 127–404	VI, 43, 1 — end of chapter (unchanged)
IX, 1–370	VII, 51, 1 — end of chapter (unchanged)
X, 1–3 (canceled)	
X, 4–62	XIX, 156, 7 — 158, 6 (unchanged)
X, 63–67 (canceled)	
X, 68–139	XIX, 158, 10 — 160, 8 (unchanged)
	IX, 77, 1 — 79, 2 (new)
X, 140–153	IX, 79, 3–21 (some addition)
X, 154–187	IX, 79, 22 — end of chapter (unchanged)
X, 188–447	XI, 84, 1 — end of chapter (unchanged)

GALLEY	BOOK
X, 448–573	XII, 92, 1 — end of chapter (unchanged)
XI, 1–12 (canceled)	
XI, 13–19	VIII, 62, 1–8 (some addition)
XI, 20–525	VIII, 62, 9 — end of chapter (unchanged)
XI, 526–645	XIII, 96, 1 — end of chapter (unchanged)
XII, 1–4	XIX, 156, 1–7 (some addition)
XII, 4–7	XIX, 158, 6–9 (unchanged)
XII, 7–25	XIV, 100, 1 — end of chapter (some addition)
XII, 26–94 (canceled)	
XII, 95–103	X, 81, 1 — 82, 21 (some addition)
XII, 104–144	X, 82, 22 — end of chapter (unchanged)
XII, 145–181 (canceled)	
XII, 182–213 (some cancellation)	XIX, 162, 8 — 163, 7 (some addition)
XII, 214–237 (canceled)	XIX, 160, 9–23 (new)
XII, 238–287	XIX, 160, 23 — 162, 7 (unchanged)
XII, 288–303 (canceled)	
XII, 304–314 (some cancellation)	XIX, 163, 7–10
XII, 315–331 (some cancellation)	XIX, 163, 11–20
XII, 332–460	XIX, 163, 21 — 167, 8 (unchanged)
XII, 461–470 (canceled)	
XII, 471–620	XIX, 167, 9 — 171, 10 (unchanged)
XII, 620–635 (canceled)	
XII, 636–733	XIX, 171, 11 — end of chapter (unchanged)
XII, 734–744 (canceled)	XX, 174, 1–17 (new)
XII, 745–809	XX, 174, 18 — 176, 20 (unchanged)
XIII, 1–501	XVIII, 132, 1 — 145, 29 (unchanged)
XIV, 1–278	XVIII, 146, 1 — 153, 13 (unchanged)
XV, 1–69	XVIII, 153, 14 — end of chapter (unchanged)
XVI, 1–371	XXI, 182, 1 — end of chapter (unchanged)
XVII, 1–48	XX, 180, 21 — end of chapter (unchanged)
XVII, 49–58 (some cancellation)	XX, 176, 20–22
XVII, 59–86	XX, 176, 23 — 177, 16 (unchanged)
	XX, 177, 17–30 (new)
XVII, 87–122 (some cancellation)	XX, 177, 31 — 178, 4
XVII, 123–189	XX, 178, 5 — 179, 28 (unchanged)
XVII, 189–206 (canceled)	
XVII, 207–221 (also see Galley XXII, 74–92)	XX, 179, 29 — 180, 20 (some addition)
XVII, 222–315	XXII, 193, 1 — 196, 4 (unchanged)
XVII, 316–321 (canceled)	
XVII, 322–448	XXII, 196, 5 — end of chapter (unchanged)
XVII, 449–465 (canceled)	
XVIII, 1–556	XXIII, 200, 1 — 215, 20 (unchanged)
XVIII, 557–565 (some cancellation)	XXIII, 215, 21–22
XVIII, 565–602	XXIII, 215, 23 — end of chapter (unchanged)
XIX, 1–619	XXIV, 217, 1 — end of chapter (unchanged)

GALLEY	BOOK
XX, 1–240	XXV, 235, 1 — 242, 2 (unchanged)
XXI, 1–373	XXV, 242, 3 — end of chapter (unchanged)
XXII, 1–74 (some cancellation)	XXVI, 253, 1 — 254, 19
XXII, 74–92 (canceled)	
XXII, 93–107	XXVI, 254, 20 — 255, 18 (some addition)
XXII, 108–225	XXVI, 255, 19 — 258, 25 (unchanged)
XXII, 225–235	XXVI, 258, 25 — end of chapter (some addition)
XXIII, 1–35	XXVII, 260, 1 — 262, 6 (some addition)
XXIII, 36–56	XXVII, 262, 6 — 262, 25 (unchanged)
XXIII, 57–62 (some cancellation)	XXVII, 262, 26–30
XXIII, 63–114	XXVII, 262, 31 — 264, 10 (unchanged)
XXIII, 115–122 (some cancellation)	XXVII, 264, 11–13
XXIII, 123–205	XXVII, 264, 14 — 266, 23 (unchanged)
XXIII, 206–208 (some cancellation)	XXVII, 266, 24–25
XXIII, 209–221	XXVII, 266, 25 — 267, 5 (unchanged)
XXIII, 222–224 (some cancellation)	XXVII, 267, 6–7
XXIII, 224–247	XXVII, 267, 7–28 (unchanged)
XXIII, 247–250 (some cancellation)	XXVII, 267, 28–29
XXIII, 250–262	XXVII, 267, 29 — 268, 8 (unchanged)
XXIII, 262–267 (some cancellation)	XXVII, 268, 8–10
XXIII, 268–280	XXVII, 268, 11–22 (unchanged)
XXIII, 281–289 (some cancellation)	XXVII, 268, 23–24
XXIII, 290–491	XXVII, 268, 25 — 274, 17 (unchanged)
XXIII, 491–519 (some cancellation)	XXVII, 274, 17 — end of chapter
XXIV, 1–239	XXVIII, 276, 1 — end of chapter (unchanged)
XXV, 1–83 (canceled)	XXIX, 284, 1 — end of chapter (new)
XXVI, 1–21 (canceled)	XXX, 290, 1 — end of chapter (new)
XXVII, 1–9 (some addition)	XXXI, 294, 1–7
	XXXI, 294, 8 — 302, 7 (new)
XXVII, 10–224	XXXI, 302, 8 — 308, 9 (unchanged)
XXVII, 225–266	XXXI, 308, 12 — end of chapter (unchanged)
XXVII, 267–268	XXXI, 308, 10–11 (italics omitted)

Textual Collation

BOOK

Chapter I, lines 1–7:

    Each time he passed the jail he would look up at the barred window, usually to see a small, pale, patient, tragic blob lying in one of the grimy interstices, or perhaps a blue wisp of tobacco smoke combing raggedly away along the spring sunshine. At first there had been a negro murderer there,

Chapter XVI, page 110, lines 1–2:

    On the day when the sheriff brought Goodwin to town, there was a negro murderer in the jail,

I, 7–43

XVI, 110, 2 —— 111, 15 (unchanged)

I, 44–54:

One day more, and he was gone. Then Goodwin could sit all day in his cell, waiting for Popeye to come and shoot him with an automatic pistol through a window not much larger than a sabre slash. Horace said:

    "Which will disappoint you most? To not be shot through that window, or to get out of this with me for your lawyer?"

    "If you'll just promise to get that kid a good newspaper grift when he's big enough to walk and make change," Goodwin said.

XVI, 111, 15 —— 122, 3:

He wouldn't talk. "I didn't do it. You know that, yourself. You know I wouldn't have. I aint going say what I think. I didn't do it. They've got to hang it on me first. Let them do that. I'm clear. But if I talk, if I say what I think or believe, I wont be clear." He was sitting on the cot in his cell. He looked up at the windows: two orifices not much larger than sabre slashes.

    "Is he that good a shot?" Benbow said. "To hit a man through one of those windows?"

    Goodwin looked at him. "Who?"

    "Popeye," Benbow said.

    "Did Popeye do it?" Goodwin said.

    "Didn't he?" Benbow said.

    "I've told all I'm going to tell. I dont have to clear myself; it's up to them to hang it on me."

    "Then what do you want with a lawyer?" Benbow said. "What do you want me to do?"

    Goodwin was not looking at him. "If you'll just promise to get the kid a good newspaper grift when he's big enough to

NOTE: Page references to the published text are to the new Modern Library edition (1966).

GALLEY	BOOK
	make change," he said.
I, 55–60	*XVI, 112, 3–7 (unchanged)*
	XVI, 112, 7–8 (new): like the children which beggars on Paris streets carry,
I, 60–68	*XVI, 112, 8–16 (unchanged)*
I, 68–70: glance, establishing by the very cunning of the workmanship the hopeless subterfuge.	*XVI, 112, 16:* glance.
I, 70–73	*XVI, 112, 16–18 (unchanged)*

I, 73–87:

with a brim and a neatly-darned veil, and each time Horace saw it he wondered again when he had last seen a veil. She wore the costume every day. The only other time he had seen her she was wearing a shapeless garment of faded calico, a battered pair of man's unlaced brogans flapping about her naked ankles, and so, although he had seen her daily now for three weeks, it seemed to him at times that he had seen her only twice in his life.

He had not noticed the veil when he first saw her in town. It was only when he returned to town on the evening of Goodwin's arrest, after he had told his sister and Miss Jenny that he had taken the case.

XVI, 112, 18–30:

with a neatly darned veil; looking at it, Benbow could not remember when he had seen one before, when women ceased to wear veils.

He took the woman to his house. They walked, she carrying the child while Benbow carried a bottle of milk and a few groceries, food in tin cans. The child still slept. "Maybe you hold it too much," he said. "Suppose we get a nurse for it."

He left her at the house and returned to town, to a telephone, and he telephoned out to his sister's, for the car. The car came for him. He told his sister and Miss Jenny about the case over the supper table.

I, 88–109

XVI, 112, 31 — 113, 18 (unchanged)

I, 109–121:

cotton-white." She nurses it too much, he thought. "Perhaps you hold it in your arms too much," he told her. "Why not get a nurse for it, so you can leave it at the hotel?" The woman said nothing, immersed immediately and without haste in one of those rapt maternal actions which any mention of the child seemed to evoke in her new surroundings. "Dont be silly," Horace said, watching her. "Dont you see they haven't got any case against him? Mark my words, three days after the trial opens he'll be able to see it as often as he wants to. More, from what I've heard about babies.—Asking

XVI, 113, 18:

cotton-white. Asking

I, 122–169

XVI, 113, 18 — 114, 30 (unchanged)

GALLEY

I, 169-182:

did.'' Miss Jenny was eighty-nine. Five years ago she had had a mild stroke. Since then she had spent her days in the wheel chair beside a window which looked down into the garden, carried up and down stairs, chair and all, by two negroes. Sometimes she slept in it. "You're going to fall out of that chair some day, doing that," they told her.

Then I'll get up and get back in it," she said. "I'm going to get up tomorrow, anyway.—And so, if I were you," she said, "I'd drive in now and take her to the hotel. It's still early."

"And go back home until

I, 182-406

II, 1-242:

At home, from his study window, he could see the grape arbor. Each spring he watched the reaffirmation of the old ferment, the green-snared promise of unease. What blossom the grape has in April and May, that is: that tortured, waxlike bleeding less of bloom than leaf, until in the late twilight of spring Little Belle's voice would seem to be the murmur of the wild and waxing grape itself. She would never say "Horace, this is Louis or Paul or whoever" but "It's just Horace," and the pale whisper of her small white dress moving in the hammock, whispering to the delicate and urgent mammalian rifeness of that curious small flesh which he did not beget. She had just got home that afternoon from school, to spend the weekend. The next morning he said:

"Honey, if you found him on the train, he probably belongs to the railroad company, and we'd better send him back. He might get fired, even. And we'd hate that."

"He's as good as you are. He goes to Tulane."

"But on the train, honey."

"I've found them in lots worse places than on the train."

"I know. So have I. But you dont bring them home, you know. You just step over them or around them and go on. You dont

BOOK

XVI, 114, 30 — 115, 3:

did.''

"If I were you," Miss Jenny said, "I'd drive back to town now and take her to the hotel and get her settled. It's not late."

"And go on back to Kinston until

XVI, 115, 3 — end of chapter (unchanged)

II, 12, 24 — 16, 8 (12, 24 — 13, 9 new):

The men returned to the porch. The woman cleared the table and carried the dishes to the kitchen. She set them on the table and she went to the box behind the stove and she stood over it for a time. Then she returned and put her own supper on a plate and sat down to the table and ate and lit a cigarette from the lamp and washed the dishes and put them away. Then she went back up the hall. She did not go out onto the porch. She stood just inside the door, listening to them talking, listening to the stranger talking and to the thick, soft sound of the jug as they passed it among themselves. "That fool," the woman said. "What does he want. . . ." She listened to the stranger's voice; a quick, faintly outlandish voice, the voice of a man given to much talk and not much else. "Not to drinking, anyway," the woman said, quiet inside the door. "He better get on to where he's going, where his women folks can take care of him."

She listened to him. "From my window I could see the grape arbor, and in the winter I could see the hammock too. But in the winter it was just the hammock. That's why we know nature is a she; because of that conspiracy between female flesh and female season. So each spring I could watch the reaffirmation of the old ferment hiding the

41

soil your slippers, you know.''

"What business is it of yours who comes to see me? You're not my father. You're just—just—''

"What? Just what?''

"Tell Mother, then! Tell her. That's what you're going to do. Tell her!''

"But on the train, honey. If he'd walked into your room in a hotel, I'd just be enraged. But on the train, I'm disgusted. Let's send him along and start over again.''

"You're a fine one to talk about finding things on the train! You're a fine one! Shrimp! Shrimp!'' Then she cried "No! No!'' flinging herself upon him in a myriad secret softnesses beneath firm young flesh and thin small bones. "I didn't mean that! Horace! Horace!'' And he could smell that delicate odor of dead flowers engendered by tears and scent, and in two mirrors he saw her secret, streaked small face watching the back of his head with pure dissimulation, forgetting that there were two mirrors.

When the swift, hard clatter of her heels ceased beyond a slammed door, he stood where she had left him between the two mirrors. In one of them he looked at a thin man in shabby mismatched clothes, with high evaporating temples beneath an untidy mist of fine, thin, unruly hair. It had never suffered ordering, though it was six years now since his wife had given over worrying him about preparations for that end.

In the window the curtains blew in and out of the sunlight in alternate fire and ash; he could smell locust on the breeze, burning along the air almost like that of full summer. It was ten degrees warmer here than in Jefferson, with that vivid, unimpeded heat of flat lands across which roads ran like plumb lines into shimmering mirage, and which lie with a quality of furious suspense even under the cold moon. Belle had chosen Kinston because of that land, the black, rich, foul, unchaste soil which seemed to engender money out of the very embrace of the air which lay flat upon it for five thousand square miles without any hill save a few

hammock; the green-snared promise of unease. What blossoms grapes have, that is. It's not much: a wild and waxlike bleeding less of bloom than leaf, hiding and hiding the hammock, until along in late May, in the twilight, her—Little Belle's—voice would be like the murmur of the wild grape itself. She never would say, 'Horace, this is Louis or Paul or Whoever' but 'It's just Horace.' Just, you see; in a little white dress in the twilight, the two of them all demure and quite alert and a little impatient. And I couldn't have felt any more foreign to her flesh if I had begot it myself.

"So this morning—no; that was four days ago; it was Thursday she got home from school and this is Tuesday—I said, 'Honey, if you found him on the train, he probably belongs to the railroad company. You cant take him from the railroad company; that's against the law, like the insulators on the poles.'

" 'He's as good as you are. He goes to Tulane.'

" 'But on a train, honey,' I said.

" 'I've found them in worse places than on the train.'

" 'I know,' I said. 'So have I. But you dont bring them home, you know. You just step over them and go on. You dont soil your slippers, you know.'

"We were in the living-room then; it was just before dinner; just the two of us in the house then. Belle had gone down town.

" 'What business is it of yours who comes to see me? You're not my father. You're just—just—'

" 'What?' I said. 'Just what?'

" 'Tell Mother, then! Tell her. That's what you're going to do. Tell her!'

" 'But on the train, honey,' I said. 'If he'd walked into your room in a hotel, I'd just kill him. But on the train, I'm disgusted. Let's send him along and start all over again.'

" 'You're a fine one to talk about finding things on the train! You're a fine one! Shrimp! Shrimp!' ''

bumps of earth which Indians had built to stand on when the River overflowed.

Once she had not been so keen about money. That was with Harry Mitchell, who never pretended to offer her anything but money, who had probably learned to believe from her that that was what she wanted and who would have given it to anyone else that asked for it; who had to build pools and tennis courts and buy a new car twice a year to get rid of what Belle had been too inert, too richly bemused in discontent, to spend. Sometimes he thought it had been because Harry had insisted on calling her Little Mother in public, sometimes because it flouted her ego to see a man's emotional life apparently fixed upon a woman of whom he could not desire, let along gain, physical satisfaction in return.

"Dont talk to me about love," she said, her eyelids smoldering, lying in a wicker chair while Harry scuttled back and forth across the tennis court, applauding all shots in his harsh jarring voice; "you're in love with your sister. What do the books call it? What sort of complex?"

"Not complex," he said. "Do you think that any relation with her could be complex?" A woman for whom even luck, life, simplified itself. Four months after his return from the war she married a man whom [sic] anyone could have known was doomed, who carried his fatality about with him, whom she had known all her life without having said four words to, or thought of half that many times save with serene and shocked distaste; three months after the wedding she was deserted; eight months later she was a mother and a widow.

"Call it what you like," Belle said. "How did she come to let you go to the war, even in the Y.M.C.A.?"

"I did the next best thing," he said. "I came back."

"Yes," Belle said. "To her. Not to me."

"Isn't one man at a time enough for you?"

"Yes. And that wont be again, Horace. Do you hear? I dont need a lover. Even though it did take a war to show me that."

"He's crazy," the woman said, motionless inside the door. The stranger's voice went on, tumbling over itself, rapid and diffuse.

"Then she was saying 'No! No!' and me holding her and she clinging to me. 'I didn't mean that! Horace! Horace!' And I was smelling the slain flowers, the delicate dead flowers and tears, and then I saw her face in the mirror. There was a mirror behind her and another behind me, and she was watching herself in the one behind me, forgetting about the other one in which I could see her face, see her watching the back of my head with pure dissimulation. That's why nature is 'she' and Progress is 'he'; nature made the grape arbor, but Progress invented the mirror."

"He's crazy," the woman said inside the door, listening.

"But that wasn't quite it. I thought that maybe the spring, or maybe being forty-three years old, had upset me. I thought that maybe I would be all right if I just had a hill to lie on for a while—It was that country. Flat and rich and foul, so that the very winds seem to engender money out of it. Like you wouldn't be suprised to find that you could turn in the leaves off the trees, into the banks for cash. That Delta. Five thousand square miles, without any hill save the bumps of dirt the Indians made to stand on when the River overflowed.

"So I thought it was just a hill I wanted; it wasn't Little Belle that set me off. Do you know what it was?"

"He is," the woman said inside the door. "Lee ought not to let—"

Benbow had not waited for any answer. "It was a rag with rouge on it. I knew I would find it before I went into Belle's room. And there it was, stuffed behind the mirror: a handkerchief where she had wiped off the surplus paint when she dressed and stuck it behind the mantel. I put it into the clothes-bag and took my hat and walked out. I had got a lift on a truck before I found that I had no money with me. That was part of it too, you see; I couldn't cash a check. I couldn't

"Did it last long enough to make you sure of that?"

She looked at him, smoldering, contemplative, relaxed in the chair. "Your impossible hair," she said. She said: "So you hope one man is enough for her too, do you?" He said nothing. "That is, if you're the man, of course." She watched him from beneath her slow lids. "Horace, what are you going to do when she marries? What will you do the night a man makes—" He rose quickly, catching up his racket.

"I think I'll play a set," he said. "Dont let that worry you. You know nothing about virginity. You've neither found it nor lost it."

Two days before her wedding he said to her: "Is there any reason why you are marrying this particular blackguard?" She was reading in bed then; he had fetched her a letter which he had forgotten at noon. She lowered the book and looked at him, her brow beneath her loose hair broader than ever, with a serene placidity like that of heroic statuary. Suddenly he began to speak at her with thin fury, watching the sense of his words accomplish steadily behind her eyes, a half sentence behind, as though he were pouring them from a distance into a vessel. "What are you, anyway? What sort of life have you led for twenty-six years, that you can lie there with the supreme and placid stupidity of a cow being milked, when two nights from now—" he ceased. She watched him while the final word completed itself behind her eyes and faded. "Narcy," he said, "dont do it, Narcy. We both wont. I'll—Listen: we both wont. You haven't gone too far that you cant, and when I think what we . . . with this house, and all it— Dont you see we cant? It's not anything to give up: you dont know, but I do. Good God, when I think . . ."

She watched him while that sentence completed itself. Then she said: "You've got the smell of her all over you. Cant you tell it?"

After her marriage she moved out to the country, to her husband's. Horace did not

get off the truck and go back to town and get some money. I couldn't do that. So I have been walking and bumming rides even since. I slept one night in a sawdust pile at a mill, one night at a negro cabin, one night in a freight car on a siding. I just wanted a hill to lie on, you see. Then I would be all right. When you marry your own wife, you start off from scratch . . . maybe scratching. When you marry somebody else's wife, you start off maybe ten years behind, from somebody else's scratch and scratching. I just wanted a hill to lie on for a while."

attend the wedding; he merely saw her walk
out of the house in a costume he had never
seen before and would never see again; he
never saw the two of them together after the
wedding.

He saw her once before her husband died.
He returned home at noon in the November
rain and opened the door and they stood
looking at one another.

"Narcy," he said, "has that surly blackguard—?"

"You fool! You fool! You haven't even
an umbrella!" she said.

In the window the curtains blew faintly
upon the smoldering breath of locust. The
house was new, of stucco. They had lived
in it seven of their ten years of the nineteen
years she had been Harry Mitchell's wife.
She had been married to Harry nine years,
and Horace thought how it had required
Harry's wife's promiscuity to render him
the affirmation of her chastity.

He walked out of the mirror and crossed
the hall quietly and looked into Belle's room.
It was pink, the bed piled high with pink
pillows frosted with lace. On the night-table
beneath a pink-shaded lamp lay a box of
chocolates and a stack of gaudy magazines.
The closet door was ajar, the symmetry of
the dressing-table broken where she had
paused again to don her hat. He went to the
table and looked. In a moment he found what
he knew he should: a soiled handkerchief
with which she had removed surplus rouge
from her mouth and stuffed between the
mirror and the wall. He carried it to the
closet and put it in a bag for soiled linen and
closed the closet and left the room.

He passed the door beyond which Little
Belle's heels had ceased. It was blank, still.
He went on and entered his study and stood
beside the flat desk beside the window.
Through it he could see the grape arbor, the
green-snared bubbles of the waxing grape,
with the sun of May stippling the small murmur of young leaves upon the floor, the light
winds talking of dogwood out of the south and
west.

On the desk sat a photograph in a silver

frame. Within the frame the small, soft face
mused in sweet chiaroscuro. He looked at it
quietly, wondering at what age a man ceases
to believe he must support a certain figure
before even the women at whose young in-
timacies he has made one: counsellor, hand-
maiden, and friend. Upon the silence there
seemed to lie the reverberant finality of the
slammed door, and he thought of Little Belle
beyond it, lying face-down on the bed probably, in that romantic despair, that dramatic
self-pity of the young.

The house was quiet. There was no sound
save a clash of metal, a slip-slop of feet on
a bare floor where a negro woman in unlaced
gymnasium shoes went about getting dinner,
the same dinner he had been eating for ten
years: only the cook was different, one of a
now anonymous succession who were not
Belle's husbands. He crossed to a book case
and took out a dog-eared volume and put it in
his pocket. From the desk he took a pipe
and tobacco pouch. Then he tried to slip the
photograph into his inside breast pocket, but
the frame was too wide. He worked it free
of the frame and it went in. From the closet
in his bedroom he took a disreputable hat of
brown felt. When he was clear of town he
crammed the hat also into his pocket, so that
the sun could reach his thinning skull.

That night he was lying in a bed of sawdust at a sawmill sixteen miles away, still
telling himself that all he wanted was a hill
to lie on for a while.

II, 243–295 (canceled):
Just a hill, he told himself, toying with that
lie, turning and turning it on his tongue until
it wore away, like a lozenge, until there
wasn't even anything left to swallow. Then
he began thinking of the house in Jefferson
forty-miles [*sic*] away, letting himself go
into the thought with that profound relaxation
of sense which is the presursor [*sic*] of
sleep, thinking of the gladioli now in bloom
upon the lawn and of the wistaria along the
eaves in thick, twisted ropes, thicker than a
man's wrist.

Later, though still aware of the black sky
cold with stars severed half overhead by a

flat roof and two thin joists, he was talking
to her. They were talking of their father and
mother, then he was telling her that he had
been dead ten years. She did not reply at
once. She merely mused above him with that
quality of utter and detached finality with
which women instinctively sift man's folly
down to the infinitesimal kernel of impossible longing and desire. She was so still that
he said:

"Oh. Was that what it was?"

"Yes. Reality is just a phenomenon of
the senses."

"Oh. . . . Where have you been then?"

"I've been at home." She leaned above
him with her broad, serene brow, the slow
dark wings of that hair which had never been
bobbed.

"How about that Sartoris blackguard?
How about him?"

Again she did not answer for a time,
seeming to communicate to him by sheer
hovering the warmth of a wisdom whose substance he himself would never touch. "Death
is just a phenomenon of the mind. A state in
which those that aren't dead." [sic]

Four days later he was within twelve
miles of Jefferson, in the hills at last,
kneeling at a spring, drinking. The night
before he told her, "There's no hurry. You
cant break into ten years like a footpad in an
alley crashing into the fatuous moment of an
oblivious pedestrian." It was afternoon. He
was walking, the coat over his arm, along an
empty road through a high desolation of
pines in which the wind drew in long, sombre
sights [sic] and where the fading crises of
dogwood glinted in the still sunny vistas,
while time, the sunny afternoon, brooded
kindly and inscrutably about him. If he got
a lift he would reach town in time to go out
to the house that night, but after not having
been passed by a car or passing a house himself in more than an hour, he left the road to
seek water.

II, 296–487:

The spring welled up from the roots of a
beech and flowed away upon a bottom of
whorled and waved sand, into willows. It

I, 3, 1 — 7, 27 (3, 1–6 new):

From beyond the screen of bushes which surrounded the spring, Popeye watched the man
drinking. A faint path led from the road to

was surrounded by a close growth of cane and cypress and gum in which broken sunlight lay sourceless and where, toward the invisible highroad which he had just quitted, a bird sang. He listened to it as he knelt his face into the reflected face in the water, hearing the bird above the cool sound of his swallowing. When he rose, the surface of the water broken into a myriad glints by the dripping aftermath of his drinking, he saw among them the shattered reflection of the straw hat.

The man was standing beyond the spring, his hands in his coat pockets, a cigarette slanted from his pallid chin. His suit was black, with a tight, high-waisted coat, his tight trousers were rolled once and clogged at the bottoms with dried mud above his mud-caked shoes. His face had a queer bloodless colour, as though seen by electric light; against the sunshot jungle, in his slanted hat and his slightly akimbo arms he had that vicious depthless quality of stamped tin.

The bird was behind him somewhere. It sang again, three bars in monotonous repetition: a sound meaningless and profound out of a following silence suspirant with the peaceful afternoon, the golden murmur of sunlight in the leaves; the very peacefulness of the sound seemed to isolate the spot, so that when another sound swelled out of the silence and rushed remotely past and died away, Horace did not recognise it: when he thought in a flashing instant of the highroad he had just left, it was as though it ran in another world, another time.

"You've got a pistol in that pocket, I suppose," he said.

Beyond the spring the man appeared to contemplate him with two knobs of soft black rubber. "I'm asking you," he said "what's that in your pocket?"

"Which pocket?" Horace lifted his hand toward the coat.

"Dont show me," the man said. "Tell me."
Horace stopped his hand. "It's a book."
"What book?"
"Just a book. The kind people read. Some people do."

the spring. Popeye watched the man—a tall, thin man, hatless, in worn gray flannel trousers and carrying a tweed coat over his arm—emerge from the path and kneel to drink from the spring.

The spring welled up at the root of a beech tree and flowed away upon a bottom of whorled and waved sand. It was surrounded by a thick growth of cane and brier, of cypress and gum in which broken sunlight lay sourceless. Somewhere, hidden and secret yet nearby, a bird sang three notes and ceased.

In the spring the drinking man leaned his face to the broken and myriad reflection of his own drinking. When he rose up he saw among them the shattered reflection of Popeye's straw hat, though he had heard no sound.

He saw, facing him across the spring, a man of under size, his hands in his coat pockets, a cigarette slanted from his chin. His suit was black, with a tight, high-waisted coat. His trousers were rolled once and caked with mud above mud-caked shoes. His face had a queer, bloodless color, as though seen by electric light; against the sunny silence, in his slanted straw hat and his slightly akimbo arms, he had that vicious depthless quality of stamped tin.

Behind him the bird sang again, three bars in monotonous repetition: a sound meaningless and profound out of a suspirant and peaceful following silence which seemed to isolate the spot, and out of which a moment later came the sound of an automobile passing along a road and dying away.

The drinking man knelt beside the spring. "You've got a pistol in that pocket, I suppose," he said.

Across the spring Popeye appeared to contemplate him with two knobs of soft black rubber. "I'm asking you," Popeye said. "What's that in your pocket?"

The other man's coat was still across his arm. He lifted his other hand toward the coat, out of one pocket of which protruded a crushed felt hat, from the other a book. "Which pocket?" he said.

"Do you read books?"

Horace's hand poised in frozen midgesture above the coat. Across the spring they looked at one another. The cigarette wreathed its faint plume across the man's face, one side of his face squinted against the smoke like a mask carved into two simultaneous expressions.

"I'm going to move my hand back like it was," Horace said. "I'm not armed. I just want to move my hand."

"Go on," the man said. His voice was cold and still, without inflection, his face squinted against the smoke. "Move it."

Later—much later, it was—the woman—she was sitting on the bed in the hotel, beside the child. It had been really sick this time and it lay rigid beneath the blanket, its arms spread in an attitude of utter exhaustion, its eyelids less than half closed, breathing with a thin, whistling sound while Horace looked down at it, marvelling at the pertinacity with which it clung to the breath which was destroying it.—The woman said: "If I had my way, I'd hang every man that makes whisky or sells it or drinks it, every God's one of them."

And he thought at the time of the two of them—Popeye and himself—facing one another across the spring. Only the water seemed to move, to have any purpose. It whispered and gurgled and wimpled on, glancing from sunlight to shadow, on and away among the willows to which it communicated a faint unceasing motion in no wind, no breath. Not only the air, but time, sunlight, silence, all appeared to stand still. The spot, the two figures facing one another decorously, were isolated out of all time: he seemed to see time become space: it was as if he looked down a swiftly diminishing tunnel upon that motion which is the world, seeing even places become a part of the rushing panorama which he would never be able to overtake.

He sat looking at the man with impotent and despairing rage. Beyond him, beyond the sunny jungle where the bird was, another car passed along the invisible road. Before

"Dont show me," Popeye said. "Tell me."

The other man stopped his hand. "It's a book."

"What book?" Popeye said.

"Just a book. The kind that people read. Some people do."

"Do you read books?" Popeye said.

The other man's hand was frozen above the coat. Across the spring they looked at one another. The cigarette wreathed its faint plume across Popeye's face, one side of his face squinted against the smoke like a mask carved into two simultaneous expressions.

From his hip pocket Popeye took a soiled handkerchief and spread it upon his heels. Then he squatted, facing the man across the spring. That was about four oclock on an afternoon in May. They squatted so, facing one another across the spring, for two hours. Now and then the bird sang back in the swamp, as though it were worked by a clock; twice more invisible automobiles passed along the highroad and died away. Again the bird sang.

"And of course you dont know the name of it," the man across the spring said. "I dont suppose you'd know a bird at all, without it was singing in a cage in a hotel lounge, or cost four dollars on a plate." Popeye said nothing. He squatted in his tight black suit, his right-hand coat pocket sagging compactly against his flank, twisting and pinching cigarettes in his little, doll-like hands, spitting into the spring. His skin had a dead, dark pallor. His nose was faintly aquiline, and he had no chin at all. His face just went away, like the face of a wax doll set too near a hot fire and forgotten. Across his vest ran a platinum chain like a spider web. "Look here," the other man said. "My name is Horace Benbow. I'm a lawyer in Kinston. I used to live in Jefferson yonder; I'm on my way there now. Anybody in this county can tell you I am harmless. If it's whiskey, I dont care how much you all make or sell or buy. I just stopped here for a drink of water All I want to do is get to town, to Jefferson."

Popeye's eyes looked like rubber knobs, like they'd give to the touch and then recover

lowering his weight to his heels Popeye had spread a soiled handkerchief carefully over them, and he squatted in his tight suit, his right hand pocket sagging compactly against his flank, twisting and pinching cigarettes in his little doll-like hands, spitting into the spring. His nose was faintly aquiline, and he had no chin at all. His face just went away, like a wax doll set too near the fire. Across his vest ran a platinum chain less coarse than a spider's skein. Behind him the bird sang again and Horace listened to it in a kind of rage, trying to remember the name by which country people knew it.

"And of course you dont know it," he said. He said: "Look here. My name is Horace Benbow. I'm a lawyer in Kinston. I used to live in Jefferson. If you know anybody around here, they can tell you I'm harmless. I dont care how much whisky you people make. I just stopped for water. All I want is to get to town."

The man's eyes looked like rubber knobs, like they'd give to the touch and then recover with the whorled smudge of the thumb on them.

"I want to reach Jefferson before dark," Horace said. "You cant keep me here like this."

Without removing the cigarette the man spat past it into the spring.

"You cant stop me like this," Horace said. "Suppose I break and run."

The man put his eyes on Horace, like rubber. "Do you want to run?"

"No," Horace said.

The man removed his eyes. "Well, dont then."

Horace heard the bird again, trying to remember the local name for it. On the invisible highroad another car passed, died away. Between them and the sound of it the sun was almost gone. From his trousers pocket the man took a dollar watch and looked at it and put it back in his pocket, loose like a coin.

Where the path from the spring joined the sandy byroad a tree had been recently felled, blocking the road. They climbed over the

with the whorled smudge of the thumb on them.

"I want to reach Jefferson before dark," Benbow said. "You cant keep me here like this."

Without removing the cigarette Popeye spat past it into the spring.

"You cant stop me like this," Benbow said. "Suppose I break and run."

Popeye put his eyes on Benbow, like rubber. "Do you want to run?"

"No," Benbow said.

Popeye removed his eyes. "Well, dont, then."

Benbow heard the bird again, trying to recall the local name for it. On the invisible highroad another car passed, died away. Between them and the sound of it the sun was almost gone. From his trousers pocket Popeye took a dollar watch and looked at it and put it back in his pocket, loose like a coin.

Where the path from the spring joined the sandy byroad a tree had been recently felled, blocking the road. They climbed over the tree and went on, the highroad now behind them. In the sand were two shallow parallel depressions, but no mark of hoof. Where the branch from the spring seeped across it Benbow saw the prints of automobile tires. Ahead of him Popeye walked, his tight suit and stiff hat all angles, like a modernistic lampstand.

The sand ceased. The road rose, curving, out of the jungle. It was almost dark. Popeye looked briefly over his shoulder. "Step out, Jack," he said.

"Why didn't we cut straight across up the hill?" Benbow said.

"Through all them trees?" Popeye said. His hat jerked in a dull, vicious gleam in the twilight as he looked down the hill where the jungle already lay like a lake of ink. "Jesus Christ."

It was almost dark. Popeye's gait had slowed. He walked now beside Benbow, and Benbow could see the continuous jerking of the hat from side to side as Popeye looked about with a sort of vicious cringing. The hat just reached Benbow's chin.

tree and went on, the highroad now behind them. In the sand were two shallow parallel depressions, but no mark of hoof. Where the branch from the spring seeped across it Horace saw the prints of automobile tires. Ahead of him the man walked, his tight suit and stiff hat all angles, like a modernistic lampstand, and Horace thought how the man seemed to know that he would not break and run, like there really was an economy of bloodshed, violence. He had never seen the pistol, yet he knew it was there just as he knew the man had a navel, and watching the other's finicking gait he thought how the man should have been a eunuch, serving his ends with a silken cord in a chamber lighted by a silver lamp of scented oil; a silent shadow high on the secret arras beyond which nightingales were singing.

The sand ceased. The road rose, curving, out of the jungle. It was almost dark. The man looked briefly over his shoulder. "Step out, Jack," he said.

"Why didn't we cut straight across up the hill?" Horace said.

"Through all them trees?" the other said. His hat jerked in a dull, vicious gleam in the twilight as he looked down the hill where the jungle already lay like a lake of ink. "Jesus Christ."

It was almost dark. The man's gait had slowed. He walked now beside Horace, and Horace could see the continuous jerking of the hat from side to side as the man looked about with a sort of vicious cringing. The hat just reached Horace's chin.

Then something, a shadow shaped with speed, stooped at them and on, leaving a rush of air upon their very faces, on a soundless feathering of taut wings, and he felt the other's whole body spring against him and his hand clawing at his coat. "It's just an owl," Horace said. "I'ts [sic] nothing but an owl." Then he said: "They call that Carolina wren a fishingbird. That's what it is. What I couldn't think of back there," with the man crouching against him, clawing at his pocket and hissing through his teeth like a cat. He smells black, Horace

Then something, a shadow shaped with speed, stooped at them and on, leaving a rush of air upon their very faces, on a soundless feathering of taut wings, and Benbow felt Popeye's whole body spring against him and his hand clawing at his coat. "It's just an owl," Benbow said. "It's nothing but an owl." Then he said: "They call that Carolina wren a fishingbird. That's what it is. What I couldn't think of back there," with Popeye crouching against him, clawing at his pocket and hissing through his teeth like a cat. He smells black, Benbow thought; he smells like that black stuff that ran out of Bovary's mouth and down upon her bridal veil when they raised her head.

A moment later, above a black, jagged mass of trees, the house lifted its stark square bulk against the failing sky.

thought; he smells like that black stuff that ran out of Bovary's mouth and down upon her bridal veil when they raised her head.

A moment later, above a black, jagged mass of trees, the house lifted its stark square bulk against the failing sky.

II, 488–495 (canceled):

It was after midnight when he left the house with the barefooted man. He found that he was drunker than he had thought, as though some quality in the darkness, the silence, the steady motion of walking, had released the alcohol which the woman, her presence, consciousness of her voice, her flesh, had held for the time in abeyance.

II, 496–638:

Just as they began to descend the hill he looked back at the gaunt ruin of the house rising above the once-formal cedar grove. The trees were massed and matted now with long abandonment; above the jagged mass the stark shape of the house rose squarely like an imperishable and battered landmark above an extinct world. There was no light in it; he could not think of the three of them— Popeye and Goodwin and the woman—as people preparing peacefully for bed and slumber, but as three figures fixed forever in the attitudes in which he had left them, waiting for him to return with the orange-stick.

The road descended gradually—an eroded scar too deep to be a road and too straight to be a ditch, gutted by winter freshets and choked with fern and bracken, with fallen leaves and branches moldering quietly above scars of ancient wheels. Horace could see broughams and victorias, French or English-made, perhaps, with delicate wheels behind sleek flicking pasterns in the mild dust, bearing women in flowered muslin and chip bonnets, their bodies rising pliant to the motion of deep springs, flanked by riders in broadcloth and wide hats, telling the month-old news of Chapultepec or Sumter across the glittering wheels. By following in his guide's footsteps he walked in a faint path where feet had worn the rotting vegeta-

II, 18, 24 — end of chapter:

Walking in single file, Tommy and Benbow descended the hill from the house, following the abandoned road. Benbow looked back. The gaunt ruin of the house rose against the sky, above the massed and matted cedars, lightless, desolate, and profound. The road was an eroded scar too deep to be a road and too straight to be a ditch, gutted by winter freshets and choked with fern and rotted leaves and branches. Following Tommy, Benbow walked in a faint path where feet had worn the rotting vegetation down to the clay. Overhead an arching hedgerow of trees thinned against the sky.

The descent increased, curving. "It was about here that we saw the owl," Benbow said.

Ahead of him Tommy guffawed. "It skeered him too, I'll be bound," he said.

"Yes," Benbow said. He followed Tommy's vague shape, trying to walk carefully, to talk carefully, with that tedious concern of drunkenness.

"I be dog if he aint the skeeriest durn *white* man I ever see," Tommy said. "Here he was comin up the path to the porch and that ere dog come out from under the house and went up and sniffed his heels, like ere a dog will, and I be dog if he didn't flinch off like it was a moccasin and him barefoot, and whupped out that little artermatic pistol and shot it dead as a door-nail. I be durn if he didn't."

tion down to the clay. Overhead an arching
hedgerow thinned against the stars to the
ultimate leaf.

The descent increase, curving. It was
about here we saw the owl . . . felt, Horace
thought. It was as though he were feeling
Popeye crouched against him, the hand between them clawing at the coat pocket. The
earth was beginning to have a tendency to
revolve on a horizontal axis just under his
feet. It was as though he were actually
walking along a sidehill none too securely
fixed; his left foot began to try to rise higher
than the other one; presently he would be
staggering. He tried to think of his sister,
of Belle. But they seemed interchangeable
now: two tiny, not distinguishable figures
like two china figurines seen backward
through a telescope. He concentrated on
walking straight, saying "This damn trouble.
All this damn trouble."

The branches thickened upon the stars,
shutting out the sky; whereupon the road itself began to grow into relief, like an inver-
sion. A moment later his feet whispered off
into sand. Against the sand he could now see
the guide—a squat, shapeless figure without
any sharpness of outline at all—moving at a
shuffling shamble like one accustomed to
walking in sand, like a mule, his feet hissing
a little in the sand, flinging it behind in thin
spurts with each inward flick of his toes.

A low shadow blobbed across the road. It
thickened, defined itself: the prone tree.
The guide climbed over it and Horace followed with gingerly concentration, hauling
himself over and through a shattered mass
of foliage not yet withered, through the scent
of recently violated wood. "Some mo of—
Kin you make hit?" the guide said, looking
back and stopping.

"I'm all right now," Horace said, getting
his balance again. They went on.

"Some mo of Popeye's doins," the guide
said. " 'Twarnt no use blockin this hyer
road. Jest fixed hit so's we'd have to walk
a mile to the house. I told him folks been
comin out hyer for fo years now, and aint
nobody bothered Lee yet. Besides gittin that

"Whose dog was it?" Horace said.

"Hit was mine," Tommy said. He
chortled. "A old dog that wouldn't hurt a
flea if hit could."

The road descended and flattened; Benbow's feet whispered into sand, walking
carefully. Against the pale sand he could
now see Tommy, moving at a shuffling shamble like a mule walks in sand, without seeming effort, his bare feet hissing, flicking the
sand back in faint spouting gusts from each
inward flick of his toes.

The bulky shadow of the felled tree
blobbed across the road. Tommy climbed
over it, and Benbow followed, still carefully,
gingerly, hauling himself through a mass of
foliage not yet withered, smelling still green.
"Some more of—" Tommy said. He turned.
"Can you make it?"

"I'm all right," Horace said. He got his
balance again. Tommy went on.

"Some more of Popeye's doins," Tommy
said. " 'Twarn't no use, blocking this road
like that. Just fixed it so we'd have to walk
a mile to the trucks. I told him folks been
coming out here to buy from Lee for four
years now, and aint nobody bothered Lee yet.
Besides gettin that car of hisn outen here
again, big as it is. But 'twarn't no stoppin
him. I be dog if he aint skeered of his own
shadow."

"I'd be scared of it too," Benbow said.
"If his shadow was mine."

Tommy guffawed, in undertone. The road
was now a black tunnel floored with the impalpable defunctive glare of the sand. "It
was about here that the path turned off to the
spring," Benbow thought, trying to discern
where the path notched into the jungle wall.
They went on.

"Who drives the truck?" Benbow said.
"Some more Memphis fellows?"

"Sho," Tommy said. "Hit's Popeye's
truck."

"Why cant those Memphis folks stay in
Memphis and let you all make your liquor in
peace?"

"That's where the money is," Tommy
said. "Aint no money in these here piddlin

car of hisn outen hyer again. But 'twarnt no stoppin him. I be dawg ef he aint skeered of his own shadow, come dark."

"I'd be scared of it too," Horace said, "if it was my shadow."

The guide guffawed, in cautious undertone. He strode on, chuckling. The road was completely sealed by a mass of growth blacker than darkness—a black tunnel floored by an impalpable defunctive glare of sand. The spring is about there, Horace thought, trying vainly to distinguish the place where the path notched the wall of tangled cane and brier. But he could feel the water there, beyond the black barrier, welling up from the tree and glinting away among the willows, and Popeye and himself facing one another across the spring while the bird whose name he could not remember sang from its still more secret place toward the ebbing sun.

"Who drives the truck?" he said. "Some more Memphis fellows?"

"Hit's Popeye's truck," the guide said.

"Why cant those Memphis thugs stay there and let you folks make your liquor in peace?"

"He's payin Lee a good price for hit," the guide said. "Takes hit offen his hands and gits hit clean outen the county."

"If I was Lee, I'd rather have a deputy sheriff around me than that fellow," Horace said.

The guide guffawed. "Oh, Popeye's all right. He's just a little cur'us." He strode on, in shapeless relief against the sand, flicking it behind with each stride. "I be dawg ef he aint a case, now, aint he?"

"Yes," Horace said. "He's all of that."

The truck waited where the sand ceased and the road, clay again, began to mount into the lost darkness of higher ground, where the trees thinned again upon the stars of more than midnight. Two men sat on the fender, smoking cigarettes.

"You took your time," one said, "didn't you? I aimed to be half way to town by now. I got a woman waiting on me."

"I bet she's doing it on her back, though," the second said. The first cursed him.

little quarts and half-a-gallons. Lee just does that for a-commodation, to pick up a extry dollar or two. It's in making a run and getting shut of it quick, where the money is."

"Oh," Benbow said. "Well, I think I'd rather starve than have that man around me."

Tommy guffawed. "Popeye's all right. He's just a little curious." He walked on, shapeless against the hushed glare of the road, the sandy road. "I be dog if he aint a case now. Aint he?"

"Yes," Benbow said. "He's all of that."

The truck was waiting where the road, clay again, began to mount toward the gravel highway. Two men sat on the fender, smoking cigarettes; overhead the trees thinned against the stars of more than midnight.

"You took your time," one of the men said. "Didn't you? I aimed to be halfway to town by now. I got a woman waiting for me."

"Sure," the other man said. "Waiting on her back." The first man cursed him.

"We come as fast as we could," Tommy said. "Whyn't you fellows hang out a lantern? If me and him had a been the Law, we'd had you, sho."

"Ah, go climb a tree, you mat-faced bastard," the first man said. They snapped their cigarettes away and got into the truck. Tommy guffawed, in undertone. Benbow turned and extended his hand.

"Goodbye," he said. "And much obliged, Mister—"

"My name's Tawmmy," the other said. His limp, calloused hand fumbled into Benbow's and pumped it solemnly once and fumbled away. He stood there, a squat shapeless figure against the faint glare of the road, while Benbow lifted his foot for the step. He stumbled, catching himself.

"Watch yourself, Doc," a voice from the cab of the truck said. Benbow got in. The second man was laying a shotgun along the back of the seat. The truck got into motion and ground terrifically up the gutted slope and into the gravelled highroad and turned toward Jefferson and Memphis.

"We come fast as he could," the guide said. "Whyn't you fellers hang out a lantern and be done with hit? Ef me and him'd a ben the Law, we'd a had you, sho."

"Ah, go climb a tree, you mat-faced bastard," the first said. They snapped their cigarettes away and got into the truck. The guide guffawed in undertone. Horace turned and extended his hand.

"Well, goodbye. And much obliged, Mister—"

"My name's Tawmmy," the guide said. His limp, calloused hand fumbled into Horace's and pumped it once, then dropped away. He stood there—a squat, shapeless figure against the glare of sand—while Horace lifted his foot for the step. He stumbled, catching himself.

"Watch yourself, Doc," a voice from the cab said. Horace got in. The second man was laying a shotgun along the back of the seat.

II, 639—675 (canceled):

The guide was still standing there when the truck roared and lurched into motion. It ground terrifically up the gutted road that joined the highway. The lights swept through the treetops, then sank and levelled away upon the yellow gravel. The wind increased, blowing upon him. He leaned into it, letting it blow upon his face and neck, looking ahead at the dark horizon beyond which Jefferson lay. The last one, he thought. It's already tomorrow.

But he had merely exchanged one unreality for another. He thought of his sister, Jefferson, peacefully, with conviction, but still it was like looking backward through a telescope. The whisky inside him was like the glare of a furnace against his skin from within, cooling away into the wind; his skin itself felt cold, detached, like the outer shell of a vacuum bottle. Presently all sense of motion ceased. The truck seemed to be suspended motionless, a motionlessness steadily vibrant against his thighs and the soles of his feet, beneath and beside which time and space rushed in a yellow band dividing a

black strip that fringed delicately off against
the motionless stars.

"I've just left my wife," he was saying.
"Just took my hat and walked out"; getting
himself across to them, with the frogs booming off in the darkness, and an owl—perhaps
the same one—and Goodwin tilted in a chair
and the halfwit squatting against the wall,
passing the jug back and forth, and Popeye
coming out now and then to smoke cigarettes
savagely beneath his slanted hat, and the
woman standing just inside the door and he
getting himself across to them, establishing
himself: "You see, I've just left my wife."

III, 1–70 (canceled):

As she had expected, he revealed no more
skill with the mop than he had with the hammer with which he had nailed the windows
down ten years ago; he realized that the
reason he was glad his sister had not stayed
was not that there was mis-understanding
between them, but that he did not want her to
see how awkward he was, thinking how women
control us not by their skill but through our
clumsiness.

"You wont stop and look on?" he said.

"I will not. If you must make a spectacle
of yourself, I dont intend to see it," she said.
She stood in the door, framed by the door
against a background of cedar-splashed sunlight. "Horace," she said. He was striking
a match to his pipe, the mop leaning against
his thigh, splashed to the knees in an island
of pale floor surrounded by damp boards,
barricaded by drying water. "You're getting
the walls all splotched," she said. "Dont
you see you cant do this?"

"It wont hurt them. They'll dry again.
Have to be done over soon, anyway."

She was watching him. "Horace." He
fanned the match out and put it carefully into
his overall pocket. "Why dont you come on
back home, Horace?" Why must you em-
barass [*sic*] me this way?"

"What will people think?" she had said
last night, when he told them what he was
going to do.

"Who'll take care of him, you mean,"
Miss Jenny said. "Let him alone. He'll go

56

on back home in a day or two, if Belle just
aint fool enough to send for him.'' She
hadn't done that. Only a wire the day after
he left: *If Horace comes there tell him I
have gone home Little Belle follows when
school is out.* "Just let him alone," Miss
Jenny said. "He dont want to be free. None
of them do. They just run out now and then
to make sure the halter is really tied. He
wouldn't come this far, even, if you didn't
let him keep that suitcase in the house. If
you want him to go back, just dont let him
come to the table at mealtime. Which you
wont do. And I wouldn't, either.''

"You think everybody's soul is in his
stomach, dont you?'' Narcissa said.

"Well, for Lord's sakes," Miss Jenny
said.

Anyway, she'll know now that I mean it,
Horace thought, sousing the mop into the
pail and swoshing it across the floor. What
I said about having the walls done over.
Nevertheless, as the mop approached the
walls he slowed it and caromed it along the
baseboard with awkward care, thinking of
that quality atrophied in him, that should
free itself in what the world called courage;
that thing which by its lack had caused him
to tell a moonshiner and a thug and a whore
why he had quit his wife and which he already
saw was on the point of sending him back to
her.

He was thinking how man's life ravels out
into half-measures, like a worn-out sock;
how he finishes his days like a refugee on a
levee, trying to keep his entrails warm and
his feet dry with cast-offs until he becomes
aware of himself, then merely furiously trying to cover his nakedness; of the sorry
pillar he runs to, the sorry post he leaves.
A shadow with an armful of feathers in a
gale, on a black plain deader than the beyond
side of the moon.

III, 71–107:

He was standing at the window beside
Miss Jenny's chair, watching his sister and
a man strolling in the garden, along the twi-
lit rows of larkspur and sweet william,
hollyhocks and tulips, callacanthus and jas-

III, 23, 1–9 and 23, 13 — 24, 2:

On the next afternoon Benbow was at his
sister's home. It was in the country, four
miles from Jefferson; the home of her husband's people. She was a widow, with a boy
ten years old, living in a big house with her

mine. Miss Jenny had brought the callacanthus and jasmine from Carolina in 1867. They were starred over with pale buds but not yet odorous.

"They cannot have walked there since last October," Horace said, "because he has changed his clothes." Narcissa was in white, the man in flannels and a blue coat.

"Who has?" Miss Jenny said. "You, Saddie."

Saddie rose from a footstool beside the chair and turned the chair to face the window.

"Ah," Miss Jenny said. "Aint the women you leave enough for you?" Horace watched the two people. "You dont expect to bring one woman another woman's leavings, do you?" Miss Jenny said.

"I dont think I expect anything," Horace said, watching the two people. "They are a little . . . They should stroll along cloisters, marble, dead shapes, not among mutational greenery. They're incongruous. Flowered walks are for young people with shy, writhing, hidden hands, walking a little blind at an interval over-discreet, while they move with the decorous precision of two figures in the frontispiece of a nineteenth-century novel. All he needs is a dyed moustache; she, one of those hermaphroditic dogs peeping above her shoulder where modern women wear artificial flowers. What is his name? the one last fall, the Virginia gentleman one, who told us at supper about how they had taught him to drink like a gentlemen—" [sic]

"Gowan Stevens?"

III, 108–140 (canceled):

"I daresay." They watched the two people move toward the front and disappear. "I dont see Bory, though. Or is Wednesday her afternoon off? . . . He and his squire were in the pasture when I passed. I waved, but they sat their steeds and regarded my passing genuflection like a couple of equestrain [sic] statues, with wreathes. But when I got out of the car they were coming up the drive about fifty yards back, Bory scrabbling along on the pony and Sundy trying to beat that mule into something more than a pro-

son and the great aunt of her husband: a woman of ninety, who lived in a wheel chair, who was known as Miss Jenny. She and Benbow were at the window, watching his sister and a young man walking in the garden. His sister had been a widow for ten years.

"But not that one," Benbow said. He looked at the two people. The man wore flannels and a blue coat; a broad plumpish young man with a swaggering air, vaguely collegiate. "She seems to like children. Maybe because she has one of her own now. Which one is that? Is that the same one she had last fall?"

"Gowan Stevens," Miss Jenny said. "You ought to remember Gowan."

III, 26, 17–27:

Through the window Benbow and Miss Jenny watched the two people, Narcissa still in white, Stevens in flannels and a blue coat, walking in the garden. "The Virginia gentleman one, who told us at supper that night about how they had taught him to drink like a gentleman. Put a beetle in alcohol, and you have a scarab; put a Mississippian in alcohol, and you have a gentleman—"

"Gowan Stevens," Miss Jenny said. They watched the two people disappear beyond the house. It was some time before he heard the two people come down the hall. When they entered, it was the boy instead of Stevens.

longed and abortive fall. He got down and
was coming in with me when Sundy reminded
him of some unfinished business somewhere,
so he mounted again. But he paused long
enough to assure me that someone would
probably show up after a while and that he
would see me later, anyway. Then he said
'Come on here, nigger' and cudgelled himself off with a flat thing like a barrel stave,
a pistol strapped at his waist, and Sundy
behind him on the mule. Which is it? are
you older than the mule, or is the mule older
than you?''

"That's the pistol Gowan gave him," Miss
Jenny said. "It hasn't got any trigger." She
said: "Do you expect her to worry very
much about a man she never bore or was
married to, when she's got one of her own to
nag and fret and worry over?''

"I dont expect anything of her," Horace
said. "She has no heart. She never had."

"You may be right," Miss Jenny said.
"The folks that wont do to suit us never
have."

III, 141–146:

"Perhaps I do expect her to do me the
constancy of being fickle," Horace said.
"Perhaps she's going to marry again, after
all." Miss Jenny said nothing. She sat so
quiet that Horace spoke again before he
realized that she had tricked him. "Do you
think she will?"

III, 147–155 (canceled):

She began to laugh, that cold, steady,
cruel laughter of old women, as though they
took a revenge on all breath. She laughed
steadily, watching him. "Go on back,
Horace," she said.

"No. I'll do Belle that constancy, at
least."

"Go on back, Horace," Miss Jenny said,
"if that's all that worries you. If you and
Bayard couldn't teach her she's well off as
a widow, I dont know what can."

III, 156–169:

She didn't talk that way last year. It was
in the early fall: again the two of them
watched Narcissa in the garden below, in a

III, 23, 10–12:

"Why hasn't she ever married again?"
Benbow said.

"I ask you," Miss Jenny said. "A young
woman needs a man."

III, 24, 3–10:

"Yes," Benbow said. "I do now. I remember last October." At that time he had
passed through Jefferson on his way home,

GALLEY

white dress, flanked on one side by a straight-backed little boy and on the other by a broad, fattish man in brown, and he asked Miss Jenny why she had never married again. More than once he had asked himself that question, telling himself she should with that complacent approbation with which you contemplate a course of conduct for another which you know he or she will not follow.

"Now, I ask you," Miss Jenny said. "A young woman like that needs a man.

III, 169–303:

There ought to be a law making them, from twenty on. They're so much pleasanter to live with. I keep on telling her that, so she wont grow into an ill-tempered old woman like me. And that boy will be needing a man, soon, if not already. Nobody but two fool women and a few darkies that let him walk right over them. . . . Will you look at that back, now?"

"Thanks," Horace said. "I thought it was his back, but I hated to . . . and he'll probably look the same from either side. Which is an advantage, I trust . . . hope." They watched the three people moving along the ordered rows where the bright, florid, dusty-odored flowers of late summer bloomed.

"Bayard Sartoris' back, to the living life," Miss Jenny said. . . . "Eh? What're you saying?"

"You'd think their mothers . . . " Horace said. "Mud bath," he said [*sic*] *"la figlia della sua mente.* She co-ordinates really too well. But I must say, that back is not familiar."

"Oh, that," Miss Jenny said. "Narcissa's young man. That's—You, Saddie."

Saddie was sitting on a footstool beside the chair. In a diminutive white cap and apron she looked like a life-size doll, a figure carved of ebony for some ceremonial make-believe. She rose and looked out the window.

"Mist Gowan Stevms," she said.

"Oh, yes; Gowan Stevens," Miss Jenny said. You wouldn't remember him. He was

BOOK

and he had stopped overnight at his sister's. Through the same window he and Miss Jenny had watched the same two people walking in the same garden, where at that time the late, bright dusty-odored flowers of October bloomed. At that time Stevens wore brown, and at that time he was new to Horace.

III, 24, 11 — 26, 16:

"He's only been coming out since he got home from Virginia last spring," Miss Jenny said. "The one then was that Jones boy; Herschell. Yes, Herschell."

"Ah," Benbow said. "An F.F.V., or just an unfortunate sojourner there?"

"At the school, the University. He went there. You don't remember him because he was still in diapers when you left Jefferson."

"Dont let Belle hear you say that," Benbow said. He watched the two people. They approached the house and disappeared beyond it. A moment later they came up the stairs and into the room. Stevens came in, with his sleek head, his plump, assured face. Miss Jenny gave him her hand and he bent fatly and kissed it.

"Getting younger and prettier every day," he said. "I was just telling Narcissa that if you'd just get up out of that chair and be my girl, she wouldn't have a chance."

"I'm going to tomorrow," Miss Jenny said. "Narcissa—"

Narcissa was a big woman, with dark hair, a broad, stupid, serene face. She was in her customary white dress. "Horace, this is Gowan Stevens," she said. "My brother, Gowan."

"How do you do, sir," Stevens said. He gave Benbow's hand a quick, hard, high, close grip. At that moment the boy, Benbow Sartoris, Benbow's nephew, came in. "I've heard of you," Stevens said.

"Gowan went to Virginia," the boy said.

"Ah," Benbow said, "I've heard of it."

hardly out of diapers when you moved away. He's a nice, well-bred young man."

"He all time sendin Miss Narcissa flouhs," Saddie chanted in treble sing-song.

"And why shouldn't he?" Miss Jenny said.

"No reason," Horace said; "no reason at all. I envy him the privilege. The privilege of not being her brother. I merely thought it was another one."

"Which other one?"

"Ay. I ask you. She seems—"

"One fo dat named Mist Herschell Jones," Saddie said.

"Thank you," Horace said, "I couldn't— She seems to keep them not only in hand, but she contrives by some means to make them friends with one another. It's like a club. I wonder if there's a grip, password. . . . No: she's like a very mature little girl playing dolls."

They watched the three people vanish beyond the corner of the house. A moment later they heard them approaching up the hall. At the door the man and the boy turned with a simultaneous and automatic deference, like to faintly insolent footmen, and flanked the door for Narcissa to enter.

"Well, Johnny," Miss Jenny said. The boy went to her chair and permitted her to touch his head with her hand. The man in brown followed, with his sleek head and his plump, young, masculine face. Miss Jenny gave him her other hand and he bent fatly and kissed it.

"Getting younger and prettier every day," he said. "I was just telling Narcissa that if you'd just get up from there and be my girl, I'd give her the air so fast she wouldn't know it."

"I'm going to get up tomorrow," Miss Jenny said. "Narcissa, why dont you—"

"I'm going to, if you'll hush long enough," Narcissa said. "Horace, this is Gowan Stevens. My brother, Gowan."

"How are you, sir?" Stevens said. He gave Horace's hand the quick, high, close grip current in eastern colleges. "Heard of you, but it's been my misfortune . . ."

"Thanks," Stevens said. "But everybody cant go to Harvard."

"Thank you," Benbow said. "It was Oxford."

"Horace is always telling folks he went to Oxford so they'll think he means the state university, and he can tell them different," Miss Jenny said.

"Gowan goes to Oxford a lot," the boy said. "He's got a jelly there. He takes her to the dances. Dont you, Gowan?"

"Right, bud," Stevens said. "A red-headed one."

"Hush, Bory," Narcissa said. She looked at her brother. "How are Belle and Little Belle?" She almost said something else, then she ceased. Yet she looked at her brother, her gaze grave and intent.

"If you keep on expecting him to run off from Belle, he will do it," Miss Jenny said. "He'll do it someday. But Narcissa wouldn't be satisfied, even then," she said. "Some women wont want a man to marry a certain woman. But all the women will be mad if he ups and leaves her."

"You hush, now," Narcissa said.

"Yes, sir," Miss Jenny said. "Horace has been bucking at the halter for some time now. But you better not run against it too hard, Horace; it might not be fastened at the other end."

Across the hall a small bell rang. Stevens and Benbow both moved toward the handle of Miss Jenny's chair. "Will you forbear, sir?" Benbow said. "Since I seem to be the guest."

"Why, Horace," Miss Jenny said. "Narcissa, will you send up to the chest in the attic and get the duelling pistols?" She turned to the boy. "And you go on ahead and tell them to strike up the music, and to have two roses ready."

"Strike up what music?" the boy said.

"There are roses on the table," Narcissa said. "Gowan sent them. Come on to supper."

"Gowan went to Virginia," the boy said. "Where my father went."

"Ah," Horace said. "I've heard of it."

"Thanks," Stevens said.

"Dont mind Horace," Miss Jenny said. "He's just jealous."

" 'Fraid that's my part," Stevens said. "But everybody cant go to Harvard. Place wouldn't hold them."

"Not Harvard," Horace said; "Oxford."

"He's always telling folks he went to Oxford so they'll think he means the State University and he can tell them different," Miss Jenny said.

"Excuse me again, then," Stevens said. "My mistake again."

"Gowan goes to Oxford a lot," the boy said. "He goes to dances there. He's got a jelly down there. Haven't you, Gowan?"

"Right, bud," Stevens said. "A red-headed one."

"Why, Gowan," Miss Jenny said. "Narcissa, do you permit—"

"He didn't go to Princeton, though," the boy said.

"Bory," Narcissa said. "How are Belle and Little Belle? You didn't—"

"Quite well," Horace said. "No. This is just a flying visit. I happened to be passing through town."

"I've been trying all afternoon to find out myself if he has run away again," Miss Jenny said. "You haven't quit Belle in three or four years now, have you?"

"Uncle Johnny went to Princeton," the boy said.

"Benbow," Narcissa said.

"And even Princeton couldn't hold him, could it?" Miss Jenny said.

Across the hall a small bell rang. Stevens, Horace and the boy went to the chair. The boy looked at Stevens, then gave way. "All right," he said, "if you want to."

Horace said to Stevens: "Will you forbear, sir? since I am the guest. As a mark of especial favor, Miss Jenny."

"Why, Horace," Miss Jenny said. "Narcissa, will you send up and get the duelling pistols from the chest in the attic?" She

extended her hand. Stevens kissed it again,
the boy watching with his bleak, light-colored
eyes. "Johnny," Miss Jenny said, "you go
on ahead and tell them to strike up the music
and tell Isom to fetch me two roses from the
garden."

"What music?" the boy said.

"There are roses on the table," Narcissa
said. "Gowan sent them. Come on to supper."

III, 304–321 (canceled):

He had not seen her again until that afternoon when he drove up to the house in a hired
car, with something of the chaotic emotions
of a bridegroom of twenty-one. It seemed to
him that he could not see in its entirety the
tawdry shabbiness of that other where a
marriage ceremony had neither promised
nor meant any new emotional experience,
since long before that hour Belle had taught
him to believe that he was merely temporarily using Harry Mitchell's body, contriving
somehow to dampen the rosy ardor of surreptitiousness with a quality turgid, conjugal
and outworn; wearing her second husband
like a lover, the lover like a garment whose
sole charm for her lay in the belief that no
other woman had one exactly like it; clinging
to a certain emotional inviolation with a determination very like prurience turned
upside down.

III, 322–335:

He sat there making no sound until he heard
her descend the stairs and saw her cross the
parlor door. Still he made no sound until
she crossed the door again and paused and
looked at him. She stood for a time, in her
white dress, with that quality of stupid
serenity upon her brow that statues have;
that quality that seemed to take him by the
shoulders as though he were a little boy and
turn him about to face himself.

"Oh, Horace," she said.

"Did you—" he said, knowing already
that she did know. "Did Belle—?"

"Of course. A wire Saturday. And this
is Tuesday. Four days. Where have you
been?"

XV, 102, 10 — 103, 15 (10–15 new):

When he arrived, there was no one about.
He entered the house and he was sitting in
the dim parlor behind the closed blinds, when
he heard his sister come down the stairs,
still unaware of his arrival. He made no
sound. She had almost crossed the parlor
door and vanished when she paused and
looked full at him, without outward surprise,
with that serene and stupid impregnability of
heroic statuary; she was in white. "Oh,
Horace," she said.

He did not rise. He sat with something of
the air of a guilty small boy. "How did
you—" he said. "Did Belle—"

"Of course. She wired me Saturday.
That you had left, and if you came here, to

GALLEY

BOOK

III, 336–347 (canceled):

He began to tell her about last night, about the woman and the child and Popeye. He could see himself talking against time, as children do, while she watched him with that expression which he realized now he had known all the time he would find. Well, I cant expect . . . he said, leaning in the failing [*sic*] window above the garden, hearing the two people come down the hall. What did I expect of her? he asked himself.

"Go on home, Horace," Miss Jenny said. "You can save your face, anyway."

tell you that she had gone back home to Kentucky and had sent for Little Belle."

"Ah, damnation," Benbow said.

"Why?" his sister said. "You want to leave home yourself, but you dont want her to leave."

He stayed at his sister's two days. She had never been given to talking, living a life of serene vegetation like perpetual corn or wheat in a sheltered garden instead of a field, and during those two days she came and went about the house with an air of tranquil and faintly ludicrous tragic disapproval.

III, 348–377:

When they came in, it was the boy instead of Stevens.

"He wouldn't stay," Narcissa said. "He's going to Oxford. There's to be a dance at the university Friday night. He has an engagement with a young lady. [*sic*]

"He'll find an ample field for gentlemanly drinking there," Horace said. "I suppose that's why he's going ahead of time."

"He kept on talking about drinking," the boy said, "until Mother said 'Are you going to drink any, Gowan?' and he said 'Do you want me not to?' and Mother said 'I dont think I would if I were you' and he kind of—"

"Bory," Narcissa said.

"Go on, Johnny," Miss Jenny said. What did he say?"

"He kind of looked at her, like he does— you know; kind of walling his eyes and breathing like this—"

"Yes, I know. I've seen him. And then what?"

"Benbow," Narcissa said.

"And he said 'But do *you* want me not to' until Mother said said [*sic*] she didn't, and he said he wouldn't, and he—"

"Benbow!" Narcissa said.

"Taking an old girl to a dance," the boy said. "He's going to Starkville to the ball game Saturday. He said he'd take me, but you wont let me go."

III, 26, 27 — 27, 6:

When they entered, it was the boy instead of Stevens.

"He wouldn't stay," Narcissa said. "He's going to Oxford. There is to be a dance at the University Friday night. He has an engagement with a young lady."

"He should find ample field for gentlemanly drinking there," Horace said. "Gentlemanly anything else. I suppose that's why he is going down ahead of time."

"Taking an old girl to a dance," the boy said. "He's going to Starkville Saturday, to the baseball game. He said he'd take me, but you wont let me go."

III, 378–589 (canceled):

Horace soused the mop into the pail and swoshed it onto the floor, watching the water

cream darkly away across the bare boards,
crested with dust so long undisturbed as to
be impervious at first even to water, crest-
ing the curled edge of the miniature flood
with pale, lace-like drifts. He was thinking
how even at forty-three a man still believes
that his frustrations should make him romantic in the eyes of other people, and how
even at a hundred he will probably still believe that the fact that he has quit one woman
should enhance his value in the eyes of
another—certainly in those of her enemy.

After supper the two negroes returned
and lifted the chair down from the platform.
It was of wood, low, with two slots in the
surface, into which the wheels of the chair
fitted, and they lifted it down and bore it up
stairs.

Miss Jenny still had a fire in the evenings. The chair faced it. Beside the chair
Saddie sat on the footstool. The boy leaned
against the mantel, his face bold in the firelight, a little sullen.

On the wall beside the bed, where one lying in the bed could look at them by turning
the head, were a number of portraits arranged in a certain order. The first was a
faded tintype in an oval frame. A bearded
face stared haughtily across the neck-cloth
of the '50's, buttoned into a frock coat. The
man was in the full flush of maturity's early
summer; the whiskers virile, the nose high-
bridged, the eyes quick-tempered and overbearing, and turning his head Horace saw a
delicate replica of it above Miss Jenny's
shawl, beneath the silver coronet of her
hair, serenely profiled by the fire, and a
shadowy, faintly sullen promise of it leaning
against the mantel. He looked at the portrait
again. Beside it hung a second and more
hasty one, made in the field: the same man
in a long gray tunic with the awry shoulder-
straps of a Confederate colonel. His trousers
were thrust into dusty boots, his gauntleted
hands rested upon the hilt of a sabre, the
bearded face shadowed by a broken plume.

"What are you doing?" Miss Jenny said.
"Looking at the Rogues' Gallery?"

65

The boy said moodily: "Gowan said he'd take me, but she wouldn't let me go."

"Why, you wouldn't leave your mother and me alone, without a man in the house, would you?" Miss Jenny said.

"Horace is here," the boy said. "Who stayed with you before I was born?"

Next was a conventional photograph dated fifteen years ago. The man was about sixty, going bald, the mouth shaded by a thick moustache, the chin clean-shaven, a little heavy. The quick temper was there too, but blurred, as though by a film, a bafflement, something.

The next was also light-stained, faintly archaic. The face was thin, dark, with dark hair above a high brow. The face above the broad collar, the puffed cravat and the high lapels of the early 1900's was that of a sick man. It was clean-shaven, haughty, young and proud.

Next was a photograph of two boys with long curls, in identical velvet suits. They were not long definitely out of babyhood, yet there was already upon the infantile chubbiness of their faces a shadow as though from the propinquity of the faces above them; a quality that utterly relegated the curls and the velvet, and already there was a distinction between them, although they were obviously twins.

The next three were in a row. The middle one was a painted miniature, the face that of a boy of seven or so.

At the fire Miss Jenny spoke. She had not moved. Her head lay back, her hands on the arms of the chair, the firelight rosy upon her. "Saddie. What are you doing?"

"Aint doin nothin, Miss Jenny."

"What does the devil find for idle hands?"

"Mischuf, Miss Jenny."

"Then what are you going to do about it?"

Horace watched Saddie go to the table and lift down a sewing basket. Squatting on the floor above it she delved into it with that intense gravity of a monkey or a coon. She replaced it and returned to the stool with a piece of coarse needlework and a dependent needle, and sat again and began to ply the needle by firelight, her head bent, tongue in cheek, her still-babyish hands moving like ink upon the white cloth, with the terrific awkwardness of a monkey or a coon.

"Yes, sir," Miss Jenny said, "I cant have any idle folks around me. If you want to be a house-nigger, that is. Or maybe you dont? maybe you want to be a field-hand and wear shoes and stockings only on Sunday?"

Saddie giggled. Bent over the work, she continued to chuckle. "Nome, Miss Jenny," she said, her voice going on in rich, dying chuckles, as though of its own accord.

"She oughtn't to try to sew in that light," Horace said. "I can hardly see her hands on the cloth, even."

"Fiddlesticks. They're part owl, anyway. Aint you, gal?"

Saddie chuckled, without looking up. "Nome, Miss Jenny. I aint no owl."

"What are you then?" Saddie bent over her slow, terrific hands, the cap crisp upon her neat pigtails. "Who made you, then?" Miss Jenny said.

"God made me. Ise a child of God." She said it in a fainting, rapturous voice; immediately she was about to chuckle again.

"You, nigger gal! Why did He make you?" Saddie hung her head above her unceasing hands. "You, nigger! Talk out!"

"For His greater glory," Saddie said.

"And who are you after that?"

"Ise a Sarto'is han'-maiden."

"Why couldn't you say so, then?" Miss Jenny turned and looked at Horace's back. "What do you think of that?"

"Habet, O most eminent republican," he said. He was looking at the miniature. The curls were still there, the eyes bold and merry, the mouth sweet. It was flanked on one side by a hasty snapshot. Both operator and subject appeared to have been moving when the camera was snapped, for the picture was both lop-sided and blurred as well as out of focus. The subject's head emerged from an elliptical manhole in a tubular affair on the side of which the effigy of a rabbit projected its painted ears into the picture. To the front arc of the pit a narrow screen

curved tightly, and two struts slanted upward
into a flat surface at right angles in horizontal perspective, from which the pistol-grip
of a machine gun tilted. The face, beneath
a wild thatch, was in the act of turning when
the camera snapped. It was full of movement, travesties [sic] by the dead celluloid,
the eyes squinted and the mouth open, as
though he were either shouting or laughing.

On the other side of the miniature was
another conventional photograph. In uniform, with orderly hair, he lounged in a
deep chair placed cleverly to bring the
subdued light onto his bleak, humorless face,
and again Horace looked toward the fire,
at the boy leaning there, at the brooding
face, the mouth emerging sullenly from
childhood, then back to the bleak eyes and
the sullen mouth in the photograph.

"Did you see the last one?" Miss Jenny
said. "Gowan snapped it."

"He went to Virginia, too," the boy said.
"But he wasn't an aviator like my father
was."

The next row consisted of nine photograps [sic] of the boy, one for each of his
years, ranging from that in which he
sprawled naked on a fur rug, through his
various avatars in rompers, velvet; as an
Indian, a cowboy, a soldier, a groomsman in
a diminutive tailcoat, to the final one in
which he sat the pony, erect, hand on hip,
a salvaged revolver-frame in his waist-band,
a small negro perched like a monkey on the
withers of a gaunt mule in the background.
This was Sundy, Saddie's twin; Saturday and
Sunday. Horace had named them: two
minute creatures with still, shiny eyes like
four shoe-buttons, born to Elnora the cook,
a tall woman in middle life who was unmarried at the time.

Narcissa entered, with a newspaper. She
drew a chair up and opened the paper and
began to read aloud, lurid accounts of arson
and adultery and homicide, in her grave contralto voice. Miss Jenny listened, her head
lying back and her eyes closed, her thin
profile rosy and serene in the firelight. Her
husband had been killed in 1862, on the

second anniversary of her wedding-day. She
had not spoken his name in sixty-seven
years.

Narcissa read on. To Horace, listening,
it seemed that they had never been so far
asunder, so completely functioning in sepa-
rate worlds, not even last night when she
and Belle had seemed for the time interchangeable. He watched her quietly, wondering what he had expected of her. He
could recapture none of it, not even the glib
words, let alone the desire.

Saddie moved quietly about, preparing the
bed. Beside it was the iron cot on which she
slept. The boy leaned against the mantel,
gazing moodily into the fire, kicking his heel
slowly with the other toe.

"Uncle Johnny was an aviator too," he
said. "They were goddam good ones."

Narcissa raised her head, her voice
stopping in mid-sentence, in shocked and
grave consternation. "Benbow! Who told
you such a thing?"

"Aunt Jenny did," the boy said. "He
said he'd take me, but you wouldn't let me
go." He brooded while his mother continued
to look at him across the suspended page.
"Taking an old girl to a dance."

III, 590–642:

At eight o'clock Narcissa took him off to
bed. Miss Jenny stirred, looked at Horace."
[*sic*]

"Go back home, Horace."

"Not home. It wasn't her I ran to. I
haven't gone to the trouble of quitting one
woman to run to the skirts of another."

"If you keep on telling yourself that,
you'll be believing it," Miss Jenny said.
"Then what'll you do?

"That'll be time to go back home,"
Horace said.

When Narcissa returned she said:

"What are you going to do, Horace?"

"I dont know. Stay here a while, I think.
In Jefferson, I mean."

"What I want to know is, why he left,"
Miss Jenny said. "I cant get him to tell me.
Did you find a man under the bed at last,
Horace?"

XV, 103, 16 — 105, 30:

After supper they sat in Miss Jenny's
room, where Narcissa would read the Memphis paper before taking the boy off to bed.
When she went out of the room, Miss Jenny
looked at Benbow.

"Go back home, Horace," she said.

"Not to Kinston," Benbow said. "I hadn't
intended to stay here, anyway. It wasn't
Narcissa I was running to. I haven't quit one
woman to run to the skirts of another."

"If you keep on telling yourself that you
may believe it, someday," Miss Jenny said.
"Then what'll you do?"

"You're right," Benbow said. "Then I'd
have to stay at home."

His sister returned. She entered the
room with a definite air. "Now for it," Benbow said. His sister had not spoken directly
to him all day.

"What are you going to do, Horace?" she

"No such luck. It was Friday, and all of a sudden I remembered how I'd have to go to the station and get that—"

"But you have been doing that for ten years," Narcissa said.

"I know. But, like I told her, I still do not like to smell shrimp."

"Was that why you left her?" Miss Jenny said. "Because you had to walk to the station once a week and carry home a box of shrimp? I always wondered why Belle never sent you back to Harry Mitchell for an automobile too, like she did for that child after she had agreed to give it up. Then you wouldn't have to walk every time you quit her. . . . It took you a long time to learn that if a woman dont make a good wife for one man, she aint very likely to for another, didn't it?"

"But to walk out just like a nigger," Narcissa said. "And then to mix yourself up with moonshiners and street-walkers. Why do you do such things, Horace?"

"Well, he's gone and left that one, too," Miss Jenny said. "Unless you're going to walk the streets with that orange-stick in your pocket until she comes to town. Are you?"

"Yes," Horace said, "out there with that gorilla in his tight suit and his straw hat, smoking his cigarettes in that ruined hall, and that filthy old man sitting in whatever chair they have put him in, waiting for them to do whatever they are going to do with him, with that immobility of the blind, like it was the backs of their eyeballs you looked at while they were listening to music you couldn't hear."

said. "You must have business of some sort there in Kinston that should be attended to."

"Even Horace must have," Miss Jenny said. "What I want to know is, why he left. Did you find a man under the bed, Horace?"

"No such luck," Benbow said. "It was Friday, and all of a sudden I knew that I could not go to the station and get that box of shrimp and—"

"But you have been doing that for ten years," his sister said.

"I know. That's how I know that I will never learn to like smelling shrimp."

"Was that why you left Belle?" Miss Jenny said. She looked at him. "It took you a long time to learn that if a woman dont make a very good wife for one man, she aint likely to for another, didn't it?"

"But to walk out just like a nigger," Narcissa said. "And to mix youself up with moonshiners and street-walkers."

"Well, he's gone and left the street-walker too," Miss Jenny said. "Unless you're going to walk the streets with that orange-stick in your pocket till she comes to town."

"Yes," Benbow said. He told again about the three of them, himself and Goodwin and Tommy sitting on the porch, drinking from the jug and talking, and Popeye lurking about the house, coming out from time to time to ask Tommy to light a lantern and go down to the barn with him and Tommy wouldn't do it and Popeye would curse him, and Tommy sitting on the floor, scouring his bare feet on the boards with a faint, hissing noise, chortling: "Aint he a sight, now?"

"You could feel the pistol on him just like you knew he had a navel," Benbow said. "He wouldn't drink, because he said it made him sick to his stomach like a dog; he wouldn't stay and talk with us; he wouldn't do anything: just lurking about, smoking his cigarettes, like a sullen and sick child.

"Goodwin and I were both talking. He had been a cavalry sergeant in the Philippines and on the Border, and in an infantry regiment in France; he never told me why he changed, transferred to the infantry and lost

BOOK

his rank. He might have killed someone,
might have deserted. He was talking about
Manila and Mexican girls, and that halfwit
chortling and glugging at the jug and shoving
it at me: 'Take some mo'; and then I knew
that the woman was just behind the door, listening to us. They are not married. I know
that just like I know that that little black man
had that flat little pistol in his coat pocket.
But she's out there, doing a nigger's work,
that's owned diamonds and automobiles too
in her day, and bought them with a harder
currency than cash. And that blind man, that
old man sitting there at the table, waiting for
somebody to feed him, with that immobility
of blind people, like it was the backs of their
eyeballs you looked at while they were hearing music you couldn't hear; that Goodwin led
out of the room and completely off the earth,
as far as I know. I never saw him again. I
never knew who he was, who he was kin to.
Maybe not to anybody. Maybe that old
Frenchman that built the house a hundred
years ago didn't want him either and just left
him there when he died or moved away.''

IV, 1–157 (canceled):
TZ he [*sic*] man had no eyelashes. At last
Horace decided what it was. At first he was
trying to remember the name by which
country people knew the joree-bird, and it
wasn't until they sat down to the supper-
table, where the lamp was, that he really
saw the man. Then the woman entered and
he was looking at her, at her hands.

Later, when he reached the hotel, he
could not go to sleep, even with all the
whisky he had drunk. He was thinking about
the woman. Now and then he would think
about the other three, the two men in muddy
overalls and week-old beards, or the slim
black one without any chin, with his quarulous [*sic*] adolescent's voice, who didn't even
drink because he said it made him sick to
his stomach like a dog and who was always
trying to get someone to light a lantern and
go some where with him; then he would be
thinking of the woman again, of her hands
putting platters of fried food on the table,
showing him her hands in that gesture half

modesty, half pride and coquetry, telling him
he might bring her an orange stick when he
returned.

When she first came into the room he
thought she was just another hill-woman,
just another of those hopeless, malaria-
ridden women he could see, barefoot, with a
snuff-stick in her mouth and half a dozen
children peeping around her skirts, in any
cabin door. But there was something about
her, something of that abject arrogance, that
mixture of arrogance and cringing beneath
all the lace and scent which he had felt when
the inmates of brothels entered the parlor in
the formal parade of shrill identical smiles
through which the old lusts and the old de-
spairs peeped; something that so definitely
postulated her femaleness, as though from
long and weary habit. Not the fact that she
belonged to that nagging disturbing inescap-
able half of the race, but that she was a
vessel about which lingered an aura of past
pleasures and a reaffirmation of future
pleasures of superior, if automatic, sort.

It was like that sense of masculine co-
ordination he got from watching an acrobat
light a cigarette or lift a fork, emphasised
by the fact that she appeared so calmly oblivious of them all save as so many mouths
to fetch food for, with the exception of
Goodwin himself, even when Horace could
hear the thug talking to her in the dark hall
while they were drinking on the porch. That
was just after he noticed her hands, before
she showed him the baby in the box behind
the stove. They had washtub, stove, all the
unending drudgery which country women
appear to accept as a part of their mammalian heritage, grained into them, yet there
was something else; something in their gestures evocative of glitter—silks, money,
jewels—and she standing at the moment in a
garment of shapeless faded calico, a pair of
unlaced man's brogans flapping about her
naked ankles. Then she went away and
Horace found the thug watching him across
the table, and he saw that the man had no
eyelashes at all.

The thug would be back there in the hall,

talking to the woman. Horace could hear the
murmur of their voices: another reason why
he believed that the woman had once been of
that half-world which had bred the man, since
she was the only one of them who appeared
able to meet him on any mutual human ground:
that trivial contact of similar experiences
which produces conversation. Then he returned to the porch and tried again to per-
suade the halfwit to get the lantern and take
him somewhere and the halfwit refused and
the thug stood there and cursed him in a cold,
savage voice and the halfwit guffawed and
Horace could hear his bare feet scuffing
slowly on the boards. The thug lit a cigarette, his face coming out of the match, and
his hooked little nose and no chin and his
slanted hat which he had not even removed
at supper, and he leaned against the wall for
a while, listening to the talk with a kind of
savage moroseness. Sulking, like a child
that's mad and stays around to show it's
mad. There was something childlike about
him: his slenderness, smallness; an air of
petulant bewilderment. But the other quality,
the thing Horace couldn't place while they
were at the spring, he didn't get until the
halfwit pointed it out. When they reached the
house the thug didn't stop. He went on into
the hall, and the halfwit said, 'Whut you let
him run around hyer in them clo'se fer?
He ought to have a pair of over-halls.
Everybody'll know he haint no business hyer.
He looks jest like a durn preacher or some-
thin.''
Whatever it was, whatever qualities he
had, they were thoroughly co-ordinated.
Horace happened to say—he'd had several
drinks by then: they had been drinking
steadily since supper, passing the jug back
and forth: Horace in a chair beside the door,
Goodwin in another tilted against a post, the
halfwit squatting against the wall. They had
got Horace a tumbler and set a bucket of
water nearby, but Goodwin and the halfwit
drank from the jug. Horace could see Goodwin's head tilted and the shape of the jug
against the sky and his long throat moving,
and he could hear the halfwit swallowing and

his bare feet scuffing slowly. Then the jug
would go thud! lightly on the floor, the liquor
sploshing up the sides in a thick, faint sigh,
and he was talking about courage, telling
them that after all it was no more than a
congenital inability to see more than one side
of any situation at one time, telling how he
seemed to have lacked it for forty-three
years, through a war and all, without knowing it; and they listening in that way country
people have, as though they wouldn't directly
put their eyes or their ears on you, lest they
seem rude. The thug came out again and lit
a cigarette, the match yellow in his hands
and on his face, and Horace talked on about
courage, trying to established [*sic*] himself
with them, and suddenly he heard his voice
saying, "You see, I've just left my wife.
Just took my hat and walked out." He was
watching the thug while he talked, as though
he were the one he must establish himself
with, and he saw that the man was really listening, as if he had forgot even himself for a
minute. Horace could see his head turned
and the cigarette coal in his hand where his
mouth had been, and he continued to tell how
he had left his wife, just walked out of the
house because he couldn't stand it any
longer. He believed that he had postulated
himself and they sat for a while in the darkness, with the owls and frogs booming away
down there in the bottom. Then the thug
moved, toward the door. "Jesus Christ,"
he said. He said it in a tone of utter and
savage weariness and went back into the
house, with his cigarette and his pistol and
his dollar watch loose in his pocket like a
coin, with the platinum chain across his
vest and a turnip-shaped silver watch which
wouldn't run on the end of it, which he had
inherited from his grandfather, with a lock
of his mother's hair in the back of the case.

   He showed the watch to Horace at the
spring, before they came to the house. Darkness had almost come when they reached the
house—

IV, 158–219:   *I, 7, 28 — 8, 20:*

a gutted ruin of a place set in a cedar grove.   The house was a gutted ruin rising gaunt
It had been a landmark for years. Horace   and stark out of a grove of unpruned cedar

GALLEY

had seen it before: the ruined monument to its builder whose name was lost with the lost dust of his anonymous bones among his neighbors—an illiterate race which had croached onto his broad domain and who for sixty years had been pulling the house down piecemeal for firewood or digging sporadically about the grounds and stables for the gold he was rumored to have buried when Grant passed through the land on his Vicksburg campaign.

Three men were sitting on the porch. The woman wasn't there. It never occurred to Horace that there would be a woman there; there was that about the bleak ruin which precluded femininity. It was like coming upon one of those antediluvian thighbones or ribcages which flout credulity by its very fragmentary majesty and from which they reconstruct an organization too grandly executed to have housed such trivial things as comfort and happiness and nagging and affection. As though whatever women had ever dwelled there had been no more than a part of the vanished pageantry of a dream; in their hoops and crinoline but the lost puppets of someone's pomp and pride, moldering peacefully now in a closet somewhere, surrounded by a faint shattering of dried and odorless petals, leaving not so much as the print of a slipper on the dusty stage. Since he had last seen it they had chopped down two of the pillars on the portico with axes, and there was a walnut newel post six feet tall and a balustrade without a single spindle left. It went half way up the wall, then it just ceased. Vanished, steps and all, leaving a faded imprint of stairs mounting the wall in ghostly progression, and in one room was a marble fireplace with the scrolled frame of an eight foot pier glass, with a few fragments of blackened mirror in the corners of the frame.

They were sitting on the porch, on the remaining end. It was almost dark; he could only tell that three people sat there. There was a light back in the hall. It was open straight through the house and he could see the roof of a barn against the sky, and then

BOOK

trees. It was a landmark, known as the Old Frenchman place, built before the Civil War; a plantation house set in the middle of a tract of land; of cotton fields and gardens and lawns long since gone back to jungle, which the people of the neighborhood had been pulling down piecemeal for firewood for fifty years or digging with secret and sporadic optimism for the gold which the builder was reputed to have buried somewhere about the place when Grant came through the county on his Vicksburg campaign.

Three men were sitting in chairs on one end of the porch. In the depths of the open hall a faint light showed. The hall went straight back through the house. Popeye mounted the steps, the three men looking at him and his companion. "Here's the professor," he said, without stopping. He entered the house, the hall. He went on and crossed the back porch and turned and entered the room where the light was. It was the kitchen. A woman stood at the stove. She wore a faded calico dress. About her naked ankles a worn pair of man's brogans, unlaced, flapped when she moved. She looked back at Popeye, then to the stove again, where a pan of meat hissed.

I, 8, 21 — end of chapter (new):
Popeye stood in the door. His hat was slanted across his face. He took a cigarette from his pocket, without producing the pack, and pinched and fretted it and put it into his mouth and snapped a match on his thumbnail. "There's a bird out front," he said.

The woman did not look around. She turned the meat. "Why tell me?" she said. "I dont serve Lee's customers."

"It's a professor," Popeye said.

The woman turned, an iron fork suspended in her hand. Behind the stove, in shadow, was a wooden box. "A what?"

"Professor," Popeye said. "He's got a book with him."

"What's he doing here?"

"I dont know. I never thought to ask. Maybe to read the book."

"He came here?"

he saw the man's car. It was parked beside the house, in the woods—a long, thick, squatting car without a top; the kind you look at with a sort of respectful awe, like one of those shells that shoot once and cost two thousand dollars. The thug mounted the broken steps. "Here's the professor," he said, and went on into the hall, toward the light. Horace could see his head in silhouette above the broken roofline of the barn, then the light came upon him and he turned and vanished through a door, the door beyond which the woman was cooking supper, with the baby in the box behind the stove. But he hadn't seen her then. He didn't even wonder who would be cooking the meal until she brought it in to the table and he saw her hands in the lamplight.

IV, 220-254 (canceled):
And while he was watching her hands he felt the thug looking at him and he raised his eyes and saw that the man had no eyelashes at all, and when he blinked something seemed to move laterally across his eyeballs, like an owl's, and Horace thought, Fancy being killed by a man you didn't know had no eyelashes, feeling the man's naked-looking eyes upon him dead as bits of soft rubber, thinking fretfully, You'd think there'd have to be a kinship between two people who looked on death at the same time, even though it was from opposite sides.

He hadn't actually seen any of them until then. He knew about what Goodwin would look like from his voice, and he had seen the second one, the halfwit, when he came up the hall with the jug before supper. He had a beautiful face, with pale eyes and a soft young beard like dirty gold. Like Christ he looked: a sort of rapt, furious face. Horace thought of form without substance, like the jet of a plumber's torch under a spell, reft of all motion and heat. He was barefoot. Horace could hear his feet on the floor, hissing a little, and whenever he drank from the jug Horace could hear them scouring slowly in an innocent and prolonged orgasm, and when the thug would quit talking to the

"I found him at the spring."

"Was he trying to find this house?"

"I dont know," Popeye said. "I never thought to ask." The woman was still looking at him. "I'll send him on to Jefferson on the truck," Popeye said. "He said he wants to go there."

"Why tell me about it?" the woman said.

"You cook. He'll want to eat."

"Yes," the woman said. She turned back to the stove. "I cook. I cook for crimps and spungs and feebs. Yes. I cook."

In the door Popeye watched her, the cigarette curling across his face. His hands were in his pockets. "You can quit. I'll take you back to Memphis Sunday. You can go to hustling again." He watched her back. "You're getting fat here. Laying off in the country. I wont tell them on Manuel Street."

The woman turned, the fork in her hand. "You bastard," she said.

"Sure," Popeye said. "I wont tell them that Ruby Lamar is down in the country, wearing a pair of Lee Goodwin's throwed-away shoes, chopping her own firewood. No. I'll tell them Lee Goodwin is big rich."

"You bastard," the woman said. "You bastard."

"Sure," Popeye said. Then he turned his head. There was a shuffling sound across the porch, then a man entered. He was stooped, in overalls. He was barefoot; it was his bare feet which they had heard. He had a sunburned thatch of hair, matted and foul. He had pale furious eyes, a short soft beard like dirty gold in color.

"I be dawg if he aint a case, now," he said.

"What do you want?" the woman said. The man in overalls didn't answer. In passing, he looked at Popeye with a glance at once secret and alert, as though he were ready to laugh. He crossed the kitchen with a shambling, bear-like gait, and still with that air of alert and gleeful secrecy, though in plain sight of them, he removed a loose board in the floor and took out a gallon jug. Popeye watched him, his forefingers in his vest, the cigarette (he had smoked it down

woman in the hall—she never came out to
the porch. She just stood inside the door
until after a while Horace was talking only at
her—; when the thug came out and cursed the
halfwit because he wouldn't light the lantern,
Horace could hear his feet rubbing on the
floor while he chortled. He never would address the thug directly; he'd talk to him in
the third person.

without once touching it with his hand) curling across his face. His expression was
savage, perhaps baleful; contemplative,
watching the man in overalls recross the
floor with a kind of alert diffidence, the jug
clumsily concealed below his flank; he was
watching Popeye, with that expression alert
and ready for mirth, until he left the room.
Again they heard his bare feet on the porch.

"Sure, Popeye said. "I wont tell them on
Manuel Street that Ruby Lamar is cooking
for a dummy and a feeb too."

"You bastard," the woman said. "You
bastard."

IV, 255–269:

"I be dawg ef he aint the skeeriest durn
white man I ever see," he said. "Hyer he
was comin up the path ther and that ere dawg
come out from under the house and went up
and sniffed his heels, like air dawg will, and
I be dawg ef he didn't flinch off like hit was a
moccasin and him barefoot, and whupped out
that artermatic and shot hit dead as a do'-
nail. I be durn ef he didn't." And he'd rub
his feet on the floor and laugh while the thug
cursed him. "Whose dog was it?" Horace
said. "Hit uz mine," the halfwit said, "a
old dawg that couldn't hurt a flea ef hit
would" and he would laugh again, scouring
his feet on the floor until the thug snarled
at him and went back into the hall where the
woman was.

*II, 19, 12–28. See above, opposite Galley II,
496–638.*

IV, 270–294:

The third man Horace did not see at all
until Goodwin came into the dining-room,
leading him by the arm. He set him in a
chair—an old man with a short, stained white
beard, who took a filthy rag from his pocket
and held it to his mouth and regurgitated
something that looked like a wad of damp
excelsior, and wadded the rag into his pocket
again. The woman brought his plate. She
set it before him, and then Horace saw that
he was blind. The others went on eating, but
he just sat there, his beard moving above
his hidden mouth. He fumbled at his plate
with an abashed, diffident air and found a
small piece of ham and began to suck it. He

II, 11, 1–14 (new):

When the woman entered the dining-room,
carrying a platter of meat, Popeye and the
man who had fetched the jug from the kitchen
and the stranger were already at a table made
by nailing three rough planks to two trestles.
Coming into the light of the lamp which sat
on the table, her face was sullen, not old;
her eyes were cold. Watching her, Benbow
did not see her look once at him as she set
the platter on the table and stood for a moment with that veiled look with which women
make a final survey of a table, and went and
stooped above an open packing case in a corner of the room and took from it another
plate and knife and fork, which she brought

mouthed at it until the woman came and rapped his knuckles, then he put it back on the plate and she cut it up for him. She cut up all his food, bread and all, and poured sorghum over it. Then Horace quit looking, but later he saw the old man open the rag again, and put the object back into his mouth. After that Horace didn't see him again. He never learned who he was nor where he went. He didn't look like any of the others; he was just there, then he was gone, leaving no gap, no hole in the pattern.

IV, 295–352 (canceled):

They returned to the porch, where the jug was, with the thug coming out from time to time and going back, and after a while Horace could feel the woman standing just inside the door behind him, listening, leaning against the door, her hands still raw with the harsh removal of grease, listening to what he was saying. He had a lot more drinks by then and he was talking again, glibly, about love and death and how a man's soul is the scoriation of his individual disasters upon the primary putty. He had had a lot of drinks, and the owls hooting and the frogs booming down there in the bottom, and the halfwit scouring his feet slowly on the floor and the thug coming out now and then. He wouldn't drink, wouldn't sit down, wouldn't anything: he just lurked sullenly and savagely about, like a sick and ill-natured child.

Goodwin sat so still in his tilted chair that after a while his immobility acquired a sort of personality. If Horace had not seen him by the lamp on the supper-table he could have told exactly how he looked, even to his brown eyes and his black head. He looked like a centurion in overalls and a blue shirt, Horace thought; like the sort of centurion who would have had a shot at the purple and probably made it go. He had been a cavalry sergeant in the Philippines and on the Border and in France. That was after he loosened up a little, talking, about Manila and the Mexican girls, and the halfwit guffawing and chortling and glugging at the jug and passing it and sayin [*sic*] "Take some mo" and the woman listening inside the door and

to the table and set before Benbow with a kind of abrupt yet unhurried finality, her sleeve brushing his shoulder.

II, 11, 15 — 12, 23:

As she was doing that, Goodwin entered. He wore muddy overalls. He had a lean, weathered face, the jaws covered by a black stubble; his hair was gray at the temples. He was leading by the arm an old man with a long white beard stained about the mouth. Benbow watched Goodwin seat the old man in a chair, where he sat obediently with that tentative and abject eagerness of a man who has but one pleasure left and whom the world can reach only through one sense, for he was both blind and deaf: a short man with a bald skull and a round, full-fleshed, rosy face in which his cataracted eyes looked like two clots of phlegm. Benbow watched him take a filthy rag from his pocket and regurgitate into the rag an almost colorless wad of what had once been chewing tobacco, and fold the rag up and put it into his pocket. The woman served his plate from the dish. The others were already eating, silently and steadily, but the old man sat there, his head bent over his plate, his beard working faintly. He fumbled at the plate with a diffident, shaking hand and found a small piece of meat and began to suck at it until the woman returned and rapped his knuckles. He put the meat back on the plate then and Benbow watched her cut up the food on the plate, meat, bread and all, and then pour sorghum over it. Then Benbow quit looking. When the meal was over, Goodwin led the old man out again. Benbow watched the two of them pass out the door and heard them go up the hall.

GALLEY

BOOK

Horace thinking, Where were you then?
When did he meet you and what could he have
said to you to fetch you out here to live like
a nigger, doing your own work, waiting for
that inevitable day when he'll be caught or
killed, and she'll have to start over again.
They were not married: he felt that; she'd
not have been standing there inside the door,
in the dark, just to be near him while they
talked. Then he realized that it was not to
be near Goodwin, but it was to listen to
Horace talking about love with a glibness
which even then could not quite obscure the
fundamental truth and tragedy which the
word evoked, understanding, since it had to
do with love, what he was talking about without hearing the words at all.

So when they told him to wait and went to
see about the truck, when he entered the
door he could feel the shock of antagonism,
awareness, coming from her in waves. He
could see the still blur of her face, motionless, like a swordsman on guard, her back
touching the wall lightly for balance, her
hands on either side, against the wall.

IV, 352–432:
He said:

"Do you like living like this? Why do you
do it? You are young yet; you could go back
to the cities and better yourself without lift-
ing more than an eyelid." She didn't move.
He could feel the awareness surrounding him,
backing up behind him like a wall, like soon
he'd not be able to move, escape, and Goodwin and the thug coming around the house
and onto the porch. "You see," he said, "I
lack courage: that was left out of me. The
machinery is here, but it wont run" and he
said: "You are young yet" and he put his
hand on her face. Still she didn't move, and
he touching her face, learning the firm flesh.
"You have your whole life before you, practically," he said. "How old are you?
You're not past thirty yet." He was saying
all this in a rushing whisper, like when there
is something that must be said and there
isn't time, but when she spoke she didn't
lower her voice at all. It wasn't loud, but
she didn't whisper.

II, 16, 9–20 (new):
"The fool," the woman said. "The poor
fool." She stood inside the door. Popeye
came through the hall from the back. He
passed her without a word and went onto the
porch.

"Come on," he said. "Let's get it
loaded." She heard the three of them go
away. She stood there. Then she heard the
stranger get unsteadily out of his chair and
cross the porch. Then she saw him, in faint
silhouette against the sky, the lesser darkness: a thin man in shapeless clothes; a
head of thinning and ill-kempt hair; and quite
drunk. "They dont make him eat right," the
woman said.

II, 16, 21 —— 18, 23:
She was motionless, leaning lightly
against the wall, he facing her. "Do you
like living like this?" he said. "Why do you
do it? You are young yet; you could go back
to the cities and better yourself without lift-
ing more than an eyelid." She didn't move,

"Why did you leave your wife?" she said.

"Because she ate shrimp," Horace said.
"I couldn't— You see, it was Friday, and I
thought how at noon I'd go to the station and
get the box off the train and walk home with
it, counting a hundred steps and changing
hands with it, and it—"

"Did you do that every day?" she said.

"No. Just on Friday. But I have done it
for ten years. And I still do not like to smell
shrimp. But I wouldn't mind that so much;
I could stand that: it's because the package
drips. All the way home it drips and drips,
until after a while I follow myself to the station, stand aside and watch Horace Benbow
take that box off the car and start home with
it, changing hands every hundred steps, and
I following him, thinking Here lies Horace
Benbow in a fading series of small stinking
spots on a Mississippi sidewalk."

"Oh," the woman said. He could hear
the deep, slow movement of her bosom, her
face still a blur against the dark wall. Then
she turned. He followed her down the hall
and across the back porch and into the kitch-
en, where the lamp sat on the table. "You'll
have to excuse the way I look," she said, as
though he had never seen her before. She
went to the stove and into the shadowed corner behind it. He didn't know what she was
about until she drew out a wooden box and
stood looking down at it, her hands hidden in
her dress. "I have to keep him in this so
the rats cant get to him," she said.

"What is it?" Horace said, approaching;
then he saw that it was a child, not a year
old, and he looked down at it without surprise
or pity or anything. "Oh," he said, "you
have a son." Then he found her watching
him with that baffling, enveloping, secret
look of women, princess or drab. From the
darkness beyond the door came voices; a
moment later the men stepped onto the
porch. The woman shoved the box back with
her knee, her hands still hidden. Goodwin
looked in the door.

"All right," he said. "Tommy'll show
you the way if you're ready."

leaning lightly against the wall, her arms
folded. "The poor, scared fool," she said.

"You see," he said, "I lack courage:
that was left out of me. The machinery is
all here, but it wont run." His hand fumbled
across her cheek. "You are young yet."
She didn't move, feeling his hand upon her
face, touching her flesh as though he were
trying to learn the shape and position of her
bones and the texture of the flesh. "You
have your whole life before you, practically.
How old are you? You're not past thirty
yet." His voice was not loud, almost a whisper.

When she spoke she did not lower her
voice at all. She had not moved, her arms
still folded across her breast. "Why did
you leave your wife?" she said.

"Because she ate shrimp," he said. "I
couldn't— You see, it was Friday, and I
thought how at noon I'd go to the station and
get the box of shrimp off the train and walk
home with it, counting a hundred steps and
changing hands with it, and it—"

"Did you do that every day?" the woman
said.

"No. Just Friday. But I have done it for
ten years, since we were married. And I
still dont like to smell shrimp. But I
wouldn't mind the carrying it home so much.
I could stand that. It's because the package
drips. All the way home it drips and drips,
until after a while I follow myself to the
station and stand aside and watch Horace
Benbow take that box off the train and start
home with it, changing hands every hundred
steps, and I following him, thinking Here lies
Horace Benbow in a fading series of small
stinking spots on a Mississippi sidewalk."

"Oh, the woman said. She breathed
quietly, her arms folded. She moved; he
gave back and followed her down the hall.
They entered the kitchen where a lamp
burned. "You'll have to excuse the way I
look," the woman said. She went to the box
behind the stove and drew it out and stood
above it, her hands hidden in the front of
her garment. Benbow stood in the middle of

GALLEY

"All right," Horace said, "I'm ready." Goodwin went on into the house. Horace turned back to the woman. "Thanks for the supper," he said. "Some day, perhaps . . . Or maybe I can do something for you in town? Send you something by the . . ."

For a moment she looked at him with that baffling, contemplative look. Then she flung her hands out for an instant and jerked them hidden again.

"You might bring me an orange-stick," she said.

BOOK

the room. "I have to keep him in the box so the rats cant get to him," she said.

"What?" Benbow said. "What is it?" He approached, where he could see into the box. It contained a sleeping child, not a year old. He looked down at the pinched face quietly.

"Oh," he said. "You have a son." They looked down at the pinched, sleeping face of the child. There came a noise outside; feet came onto the back porch. The woman shoved the box back into the corner with her knee as Goodwin entered.

"All right," Goodwin said. "Tommy'll show you the way to the truck." He went away, on into the house.

Benbow looked at the woman. Her hands were still wrapped into her dress. "Thank you for the supper," he said. "Some day, maybe . . ." He looked at her; she was watching him, her face not sullen so much, as cold, still. "Maybe I can do something for you in Jefferson. Send you something you need . . ."

She removed her hands from the fold of the dress in a turning, flicking motion; jerked them hidden again. "With all this dishwater and washing . . . You might send me an orange-stick," she said.

V, 1

V, 2–146 (canceled):
After that first evening she did not mention Belle, Kinston, made no reference to any future, yet as he watched the familiar motions of her hands and body and listened to the familiar sound of her voice as they talked of trivial things, of their childhood, their surroundings, it seemed to him that they had never been so far asunder. He was watching a stranger, a usurper wearing the garments of someone that had died. There was no strife, antagonism, conflict. There was nothing. The gestures she made, the words she spoke, had no significance. They were not spoken to him, had no relation to his past or present.

He wondered if deserting Belle had altered him, had inculcated him with some quality of

XV, 103, 10 (unchanged)

XV, 103, 10–15 (new). See above, opposite Galley III, 322–335.

falseness which made false all whom he approached. He thought of returning to her and
found that he could contemplate it without any
emotion whatever save that of a faint reluc-
tance toward the effort of overcoming a
primary inertia. He thought of the woman in
the calico dress, of the evening he had spent
there, wondering if perhaps that had changed
him; if perhaps he had become leavened with
a reality which had completely destroyed a
world of illusion which he had thought for
forty-three years was real.

In the forenoons he read, or talked with
Miss Jenny of his sister, in the afternoons
he rambled about the farm with the boy and
Sundy; after supper Narcissa read the Memphis paper aloud in Miss Jenny's room.
Then he would go to his room, where the
suitcase stayed in the locked closet, where
Little Belle's photograph was propped against
a book on the table. He stood for a while before it, looking at the soft, sweet, vague face,
thinking quietly how even at forty-three a
man . . . that incomprehensible conviction of
aging flesh that respect is due that common-
est phenomenon in life: an accumulation of
hours, breaths, temporarily in a single im-
permanent clot. Then he would go to bed, to
lie in the darkness while the scents from the
garden came up from below upon the soft,
dark, blowing air, not thinking of anything at
all.

He seemed to have expected her to be impervious not only to marriage, but to Sar-
torises as well. Yet even as the car entered
the drive that led up to the square white
house in its park of locusts and oaks, entering that atmosphere with which four generations of cold-blooded men clinging violently
to their outworn traditions of human behavior
had imbued the very soil on which they had
lived, he was saying Damn that brute. Damn
that brute. And later, pushing the mop back
and forth with an awkward and ludicrous es-
capement of approximately enough energy to
gin a bale of cotton, he thought of his sister
as a figure enchanted out of all time between
a bed-ridden old woman eighty-nine years
old who summed in her person the ultimate

frustration of all the furious folly of that
race, and a nine-year-old boy emerging full-
fledged from the soft haze of childhood into a
tradition that had violently slain three men
in four generations while in the throes of its
own rigor-mortis. He had expected a woman
to follow a man whom she had neither married nor borne, into that region of truth
divorced from all reality which no woman is
fool enough to assay; to follow the very man
who had just repudiated that region of reality
divorced from truth which women accept and
make liveable.

On the second night he dreamed that he
was a boy again and waked himself crying in
a paroxysm of homesickness like that of a
child away from home at night, alone in a
strange room. It seemed to him that not only
the past two days, but the last thirty-five
years had been a dream, and he waked himself calling his mother's name in a paroxysm
of terror and grief.

He was afraid to turn on the light. Sitting
there in the bed in the dark, he believed that
he had irrevocably lost something, but he
believed that if he turned on the light, he
would lose even the sense, the knowledge of
his loss. So he sat there, hugging his knees,
not crying any longer.

After a while he could not tell whether he
were awake or not. He could still sense a
faint motion of curtains in the dark window
and the garden smells, but he was talking to
his mother too, who had been dead thirty
years. She had been an invalid, but now she
was well; she seemed to emanate that abound-
ing serenity as of earth which his sister had
done since her marriage and the birth of her
child, and she sat on the side of the bed, talking to him. With her hands, her touch, because he realised that she had not opened her
mouth. Then he saw that she wore a shapeless garment of faded calico and that Belle's
rich, full mouth burned sullenly out of the
halflight, and he knew that she was about to
open her mouth and he tried to scream at her,
to clap his hand to her mouth. But it was too
late. He saw her mouth open; a thick, black
liquid welled in a bursting bubble that splayed

out upon her fading chin and the sun was shining on his face and he was thinking He smells
black. He smells like that black stuff that
ran out of Bovary's mouth when they raised
her head.

He rose and dressed and went down. For
an hour he walked up and down the porch
before the breakfast bell rang. Narcissa and
the boy were at the table.

"I'm going home," he said. "I want the
key."

"I knew you would have . . ." He watched
the sentence, the sense, take shape behind
her eyes, a half-sentence late, as usual.
"The key?"

"To the house," he said. "I'm going
home."

The house was of red brick, set above a
sloping lawn where gladioli bloomed at random in the uncut grass that year after year
had gone rankly and lustily to seed. You entered a wrought-iron gate in a fence massed
with honeysuckle, from which the cedar-
bordered drive rose and curved in a half-
moon. The cedars needed pruning too, their
dark tips a jagged mass like a black wave
breaking without foam upon the May sky,
breaking on against the house itself in a fixed
whelming surge.

Along the once white eaves thick, twisted
ropes of wistaria grew. Beneath the vine a
lilac snow of petals lay upon the dark earth
of an unturned flower bed where a few sere
canna stalks rose from a blanket of anonymous mold. The gutters were choked with
molded vegetation also, in which grass seed
and even acorns had sprouted, sagging beneath the accumulated weight and in two
places broken, staining the bricks with dark
streaks.

V. 147–152:

He and his sister had been born in it,
seven years apart. It had been closed for
ten years, since his sister's marriage and
since the day he had moved away to live with
Belle in a rented house in Kinston, until they
built the stucco bungalow,

XV, 102, 1–9:

Benbow reached his sister's home in the
middle of the afternoon. It was four miles
from town, Jefferson. He and his sister were
born in Jefferson, seven years apart, in a
house which they still owned, though his sister had wanted to sell the house when Ben-

GALLEY

BOOK

V, 152-235 (canceled):
yet as he moved about the tight and inscrutable desolation in a prolonged orgasm of
sentimental loneliness, he seemed to hurdle
time and surprise his sister and himself in
a thousand forgotten pictures out of the
serene fury of their childhood as though it
had been no longer ago than yesterday,
evoked sometimes by no more than a brace-
let of rotting rope, a scarce-distinguishable
knot healed into a limb and become one with
the living wood.

The windows were as he had nailed them
up ten years ago. The nails were clumsily
driven, since he had had no more skill with
that lost hammer than he expected to reveal
with the mop and broom which, with a feeling
of humility, immolation, he had ordered.
Rusted, mute, the warped and battered heads
emerged from the wood or lay hammered
flat into it by clumsy blows. From each one
depended a small rusty stain, like a dried
tear or a drop of blood; he touched them,
drawing his finger across the abrasions. "I
crucified more than me, then," he said aloud.

At ten o'clock a light truck whirled in the
gate and rushed up the drive and slewed to a
halt at the front door. A hatless white youth
began to hurl packages onto the porch. He
took a cigarette from behind his ear and
borrowed a match from Horace and snatched
the truck about and rushed away.

The parcels lay helter-skelter along the
porch. Horace gathered them up and opened
them until he came upon a small bottle of oil.
He oiled the lock and the rusty key and opened
the door. He carried the things in—a broom,
a mop; pails; a suit of overalls; a hammer.
He donned the overalls and opened the doors
upon peaceful dust. With the hammer he
drew the nails in the shutters and opened the
windows and let in the bright air, going from
room to room. It seemed to him that he
came upon himself and his sister, upon their
father and mother, who had been an invalid
so long that the one picture of her he re-
tained was two frail arms rising from a soft
falling of lace, moving delicately to an inter-
minable manipulation of colored silk, in

bow married the divorced wife of a man
named Mitchell and moved to Kinston. Benbow would not agree to sell, though he had
built a new bungalow in Kinston on borrowed
money upon which he was still paying interest.

fading familiar gestures in the instant between darkness and sunlight. Then he filled
the pail and began to scrub the floors, finding that awkwardness which he had antici-
pated, stopping now and then to stretch his
muscles, falling to work again.

At noon he removed the overalls and went
down town. A bell was ringing inside the
hotel, and the drummers were quitting the
chairs along the locust-shaded curb and
moving toward the door, but he didn't stop.
In a delicatessen he bought tinned meat and
crackers, in the soda-fountain a bottle of
milk. He purchased a pair of sheets and a
blanket and returned home and ate his lunch
from a newspaper on the kitchen table. The
newspaper was brown and faded, dated
Memphis, Tenn., Aug. 27, 1919. He turned
it over, munching the final cracker. His
sister's face looked back at him, the print
blurred and discolored. In the corner of the
picture a smaller photograph, a reproduc-
tion of the one on Miss Jenny's wall, was
inset. Above was a decorous caption: Mississippi Bride, and beneath: . . . *of Jefferson, to Captain Bayard Sartoris*. He looked
at the picture, chewing slowly, asking himself what he had expected of her. When he
remembered word for word their talks during the four nights between Kinston and
Jefferson, it seemed to him that she had
lied to him deliberately, leaning above him
with that serene and constant dullness which
could not even have assimilated, let alone
phrased, the very thoughts which she had
voiced. Telling him that reality is just
phenomenon [*sic*] of the senses. Maybe it's
because women are wise enough to be moved
only by the evocation of the words, while
only men insist upon the sense.

V, 236–247:

　　At six she returned in the car.

"Come on home, Horace. Dont you see
you cant do this?"

"I realized that when I started," he said.
"Until this morning I thought that anyone
with one arm and a pail of water could mop
a floor."

"Horace."

XV, 106, 1–18:

　　The next morning Benbow got the key to
the house from his sister, and went into
town. The house was on a side street, un-
occupied now for ten years. He opened the
house, drawing the nails from the windows.
The furniture had not been moved. In a pair
of new overalls, with mops and pails, he
scoured the floors. At noon he went down

"I'm going to stay here. I have covers."
Suddenly he said: "I'm the oldest, remember."

He went to the hotel for supper and returned in the twilight.

V, 247–292 (canceled):
In the center of the lawn, equidistant from either wing of the drive, between house and fence, was an oak. It was old and thick and squat, impenetrable to sun or rain. It was circled by a crude wooden bench, onto the planks of which the bole, like breasts of that pneumatic constancy so remote from lungs as to be untroubled by breath, had croached and over-bosomed until supporting trestles were no longer necessary. He sat on the bench, smoking, his back against the tree, remembering how on summer afternoons, all four of them would sit there while the spent summer rain murmured among the leaves and the thick breath of the honeysuckle bore up the slope in rich gusts, and usually a mockingbird somewhere in the peaceful twilight-colored rain already broken to the westward by a yellow wash of dying sunlight.

He was thinking how women seem not to have associations at all. Perhaps it is because she lives here and can see it everyday, he thought. But then he remembered how Belle not only would not return to Jefferson, but spoke of it and the people with a sort of vindictiveness, as a victim of outrage, which she could somehow make quite personal and foist upon him as though he had created the town and its inhabitants. Perhaps it's trees that affect her so, he thought, thinking of the stucco bungalow set in its treeless lawn, of Belle on the porch watching him with brooding impatience as he watered the maple and cottonwood seedlings which he had set out. Perhaps she lived among too many trees before, thinking of the house where she had lived with Harry Mitchell. It was two streets away from where he sat—a horrible travesty in scrolled and tortured wood and metal, set in a lawn of regal proportions, among oaks under which Grant's infantry had bivouacked, and he remembered

town and bought bedding and some tinned food. He was still at work at six o'clock when his sister drove up in her car.

"Come on home, Horace," she said. "Dont you see you cant do this?"

"I found that out right after I started," Benbow said. "Until this morning I thought that anybody with one arm and a pail of water could wash a floor."

"Horace," she said.

"I'm the older, remember," he said. "I'm going to stay here. I have some covers." He went to the hotel for supper

that quality passionate and strange with which
she had invested it, gargoyles and scrolls
and all, as she moved there in a series of
pictures rich with sullen promise; thinking
of that aura of voluptuous promise with which
sheer discontent can invest another's wife.

V, 293–297:

   At eight oclock Isom drove in. He had a
big bundle. "Miss Narcissa say fer you to
use them," he said. It was bed-clothing.
He put it carefully away and made the bed
with those which he had bought.

XV, 106, 18–23:

When he returned, his sister's car was again
in the drive. The Negro driver had brought a
bundle of bedclothing.

   "Miss Narcissa say for you to use them,"
the Negro said. Benbow put the bundle in a
closet and made a bed with the ones which he
had bought.

V, 298–355 (canceled):

   Just before he went to sleep he was thinking of the woman in the calico garment, of
himself and Goodwin and the halfwit sitting
with the jug on the porch; of how, having
blundered into that reality which he thought
he was so hot for, his efforts to establish
himself as a factor in it had been like those
of a boy watching other boys do things he
cannot or dare not attempt, and who performs
the dwarfed mimicry of their skill or daring
with a sort of raging importunity: Look at
me! Look at me! Telling one man who had
roughly brushed aside all the triviata of
registered vows to carry the woman into
what was practically a state of servitude,
and another man who appeared to have dis-
pensed even with love with a savage finality,
that he had left his wife, who couldn't stay
married even in that ultimate apotheosis of
vegetable comfort which keeps us good from
habit: a stucco bungalow. Talking glibly to
a woman who had run the gamut of love between galley-bench and calvary, of love, who
knew it only as a dead parade of words across
dead paper in which was tombed, as though
it were a new and terrible thing, some anonymous one's final baffled and bitter plaint
against time and death and the springing
blood and sweat.

   "You see, I left my wife," he said, trying
to establish himself, get himself across to
them, and the woman standing there in the
dark hall, just inside the door, listening. As

soon as he said it he was wondering if he
were trying to establish himself with them
or with himself; if he were not trying to
complete the gesture of desertion by telling
another woman of it as soon as possible; if
that were not necessary always, since ascetic
men never seem to quit their wives: thinking
that if there were no other women in the
world a man would not quit his wife for more
reasons than one. It was marriage they were
trying to quit, since any woman makes a
better mistress than she does a wife. And
for the man who marries his mistress there
is but one excuse: she was the woman of the
two.

"I've just left my wife," he said; "just
took my hat and walked out"; and the frogs
booming away in the bottom, and Goodwin in
his tilted chair and the halfwit squatting
against the wall with that timeless patience
of country people or crucifixes, and Popeye
coming out from time to time to smoke
cigarettes savagely under the vicious slant
of his hat. Just inside the door the woman
stood; he could feel her there: a steady
postulate of female flesh with which he was
trying to establish that dumb spark of the
universal truth which each man carries inside the slowly hardening shell of his secret
breath, into a solitary grave.

V, 356–372   *XV, 106, 24 — 107, 8 (unchanged)*

V, 373–407 (canceled):

Across the street and some distance away,
a frame house stood in a lawn of big oaks. It
was in need of paint, covered with intricate
scrolls of tortured wood and iron. The lawn
was cut by wheel-marks and almost grass-
less, the earthen space between street and
house a series of ruts filled with ashes and
broken bricks. Along the curb stood a line
of cars. Three others stood on the lawn,
clay-splashed, bearing mud-crusted, transient license-plates. Along the veranda-
railing a row of boot-soles faced the street.
Nailed to a tree near the street was a
weathered sign: Rooms & Meals. Horace
stood across the street, looking at it, the
anonymous cars, the feet, the air of furious

and transient promiscuity which now invested
it; thinking of Little Belle with her round,
soft head, in a small colored dress, upon the
lawn; of Belle's unseen presence already
felt as he would enter the gate; thinking of
Harry with his harsh, jarring voice, his
scuttling, short-legged gait, his boy-like
innocent pride in his possessions—the new
car or gun or tennis racket which he would
give you if you asked for it, regarding your
gratitude or not gratitude with that sad, baffled thing in his eyes that bulldogs have;
give you his wife, his child.

  Big Boy, I'll say—I'll have to say Big
Boy—It's like this: I thought I wanted your
wife, but I seem to have been mistaken. So
I've got to find someone I know will be good
to her, you see. So I said, Big Boy here will
be the man, the man in a thousand, ten thousand . . . I'll have to say Big Boy, he thought,
walking swiftly toward the square.

V, 407–475   *XV, 107, 8 — end of chapter (unchanged)*

VI, 1–23   *XVII, 122, 1 — 123, 2 (unchanged)*

VI, 24–28 (canceled):

  "Damn that fellow!" Goodwin said, jerking his head up restively, rolling a cigarette
from the cloth sack between his teeth. Beside him the woman sat on the cot, the child
on her lap. Beside her the gray hat lay, set
carefully aside.

VI, 29–32:   *XVII, 123, 3–9 (3–7 new):*

Heretofore the child had lain in a drugged-   Each morning Isom fetched in a bottle of
like apathy, its eyelids closed to a thin   milk, which Horace delivered to the woman
crescent, but today it moved now and then in   at the hotel, for the child. On Sunday after-
frail, galvanic jerks, whimpering.   noon he went out to his sister's. He left the
                                                 woman sitting on the cot in Goodwin's cell,
                                                 the child on her lap. Heretofore it had lain
                                                 in that drugged apathy, its eyelids closed to
                                                 thin crescents, but today it moved now and
                                                 then in frail, galvanic jerks, whimpering.

VI, 33–67:   *XVII, 123, 10 — 124, 4:*

  "Hush," the woman said, rocking it on   Horace went up to Miss Jenny's room.
her knees, "shhhhhhhhhhh."   His sister had not appeared. "He wont talk,"
  "I tell you, they've got nothing on me,"   Horace said. "He just says they will have to
Goodwin said. "They've got no more on me   prove he did it. He said they had nothing on
than they have on her, on that kid."   him, no more than on the child. He wouldn't
  He had waived bond. "He said he was   even consider bond, if he could have got it.

GALLEY

better off there," Horace told Miss Jenny.
That was at Sunday dinner. Then suddenly
he was living out there again. He could not
have told himself how it happened. But all
at once he realised that he had returned, not
to that which he had walked all the way from
Kinston to Jefferson to find, but to a certain
amicable arrangement of communal sleeping
and eating in which all those engaged were
aware that where you ate and slept was not
important. He thought his reason was to be
near a telephone and have the use of a car.
Miss Jenny thought it was because of the
food. "And I suppose he is," he said. "His
business out yonder is finished, even if they
hadn't found his kettle and des—"

"Kettle?" Miss Jenny said.

"His still. They hunted around until they
found it before they brought him in. Once he
was down, you see, they all jumped on him.
All his good customers that had been buying
from him and drinking what he'd give them
free and trying to make love to her behind
his back. You should hear them down town.
Sunday the Baptist minister took him for a
text, and her too. Good God, can a man seriously voice the statement that by bringing
a child into the world a woman can have put
a noose about the neck of the man who begot
it?"

VI, 68–164

VI, 165–179

VI, 180–198 (canceled):

"She's jealous," Horace said. Miss
Jenny looked at him, her gray eyes cold and
keen. During the year before his sister's
marriage she had received a series of anonymous love-letters written by a scarce
literate man. Inarticulate, obscene and sincere, she read them with detached equanimity, seeming to have no curiosity whatever
regarding the author, not even bothering to
destroy them. One night they were stolen:

BOOK

He says he is better off in the jail. And I
suppose he is. His business out there is
finished now, even if the sheriff hadn't found
his kettles and destroyed—"

"Kettles?"

"His still. After he surrendered, they
hunted around until they found the still. They
knew what he was doing, but they waited until
he was down. Then they all jumped on him.
The good customers, that had been buying
whiskey from him and drinking all that he
would give them free and maybe trying to
make love to his wife behind his back. You
should hear them down town. This morning
the Baptist minister took him for a text. Not
only as a murderer, but as an adulterer; a
polluter of the free Democratico-Protestant
atmosphere of Yoknapatawpha county. I
gathered that his idea was that Goodwin and
the woman should both be burned as a sole
example to that child; the child to be reared
and taught the English language for the sole
end of being taught that it was begot in sin
by two people who suffered by fire for having
begot it. Good God, can a man, a civilised
man, seriously . . . ."

XVII, 124, 5 — 126, 23 (unchanged)

XVII, 126, 24–25 (new):
Horace read the note, the single sheet.
He held it between his hands. He did not say
anything for a while.

XVII, 126, 26 — 127, 7 (unchanged)

91

that was the only time Horace ever saw her
lose her poise. He saw her then in the
throes of a passion nearer maternal than
actual motherhood ever roused; not with
outrage or fear, but at the idea of having
letters addressed to her read by someone
she did not know.

Miss Jenny was watching him. "She's
jealous," he said.

"And you're saying to yourself, That's
something. Aint you?" she said.

XVII, 127, 8–17 (new):

"I'll know whether or not I have any
backbone when you tell me what the other
way is."

"Go back to Belle," Miss Jenny said.
"Go back home."

The Negro murderer was to be hanged on
a Saturday without pomp, buried without cir-
cumstance: one night he would be singing at
the barred window and yelling down out of
the soft myriad darkness of a May night; the
next night he would be gone, leaving the window for Goodwin. Goodwin had been bound
over for the June term of court, without bail.

XVII, 127, 17 — 130, 8 (unchanged)

VI, 199–298

VI, 299–314 (canceled):

After supper he went to Miss Jenny's
room. He drew a chair up and sat down and
began to fill his pipe. He filled it slowly, as
though he were not conscious of his hands.

"Well," Miss Jenny said, "how's it going?"

"What?" he said. "Oh. All right. All
right."

"That woman, I mean. A hotel's no place
for a young baby. That bottle of milk you
carry in, that's not enough. I'd like to see
her."

"I wish you could. But Narcissa—"

"I thought you might bring her out to supper some night."

"Yes. Some night." He lit the pipe, then
he let it go out again, staring at the fire.

"You might get your spunk up and try it,
anyway."

"Yes," he said. He moved suddenly.

GALLEY

BOOK

XVII, 130, 9–14 (new):
That night Horace built a small fire in the grate. It was not cool. He was using only one room now, taking his meals at the hotel; the rest of the house was locked again. He tried to read, then he gave up and undressed and went to bed, watching the fire die in the grate. He heard the town clock strike twelve.

VI, 315–317

XVII, 130, 14–16 (unchanged)

VI, 318–321 (canceled):
At his window, undressed, the light off, he could smell the garden, the myriad earth, the myriad darkness. By God I will go, he said; I'll write Belle in the morning.

VI, 321–354:
They would be gathered along the fence, now, and the thick, small-headed shape of the negro clinging to the bars, gorilla-like, beneath the ragged grieving of the heaven-tree between the light, the last bloof [*sic*] fallen now in viscid smears. "They ought to clean that mess off the walk," he said. Damn, damn, damn.

The next morning Saddie knocked on his door before he was up. "Miss Jenny say fer you to come to her room."

He slipped on his robe and found Miss Jenny propped in bed, a woolen shawl about her shoulders. Beside the bad [*sic*] a desk telephone sat on the table. After her stroke the extension had been made from the instrument downstairs.

"You're in trouble," she said. "Your family."

"Was it Belle? What—"

"Your pistol widow. I couldn't get her to wait. She wants you in a hurry. She didn't say so, but she wants you to come right away. You might try to call her back. Saddie, bring a chair for Mr Horace."

"No," Horace said, "I'll go on in. I'll get some breakfast in town. Saddie [*sic*] will you run and ask Isom to get the car out?"

"Why not call her and find out what it is?" Miss Jenny said. "I like her voice."

"I'll have to go in, anyway."

"Then I'll have to wait until tonight to find out what it is, wont I?" Miss Jenny said.

XVII, 130, 17 — 131, 2:
Maybe a few of them would still be gathered along the fence, since this would be his last night; the thick, small-headed shape of him would be clinging to the bars, gorilla-like, singing, while upon his shadow, upon the checkered orifice of the window, the ragged grief of the heaven tree would pulse and change, the last bloom fallen now in viscid smears upon the sidewalk. Horace turned again in the bed. "They ought to clean that damn mess off the sidewalk," he said. "Damn. Damn. Damn."

He was sleeping late the next morning; he had seen daylight. He was wakened by someone knocking at the door. It was half-past six. He went to the door. The Negro porter of the hotel stood there.

"What?" Horace said. "Is it Mrs Goodwin?"

"She say for you to come when you up," the Negro said.

"Tell her I'll be there in ten minutes."

GALLEY

BOOK

"I'm afraid so," he said.

He dressed rapidly, without stopping to shave.

VI, 355–372

VII, 1–397

VIII, 1–126

VIII, 127–404

IX, 1–370

X, 1–3 (canceled):

Tm he [*sic*] woman leaned above the child, her face bent toward it in a musing attitude, as though she were not seeing it.

X, 4–62

X, 63–67 (canceled):
Deep full her bosom moved under the gray crepe. Horace watched her, the down-turned cheek, the hair bobbed once but drawn now to a knot at the back, at one rigid arm and the slow clenching of her hands in her lap.

X, 68–139

XVII, 131, 3 — end of chapter (unchanged)

IV, 28, 1 — end of chapter (unchanged)

V, 39, 1 — end of chapter (unchanged)

VI, 43, 1 — end of chapter (unchanged)

VII, 51, 1 — end of chapter (unchanged)

XIX, 156, 7 — 158, 6 (unchanged)

XIX, 158, 10 — 160, 8 (unchanged)

IX, 77, 1 — 79, 2 (new):
The room was dark. The woman stood inside the door, against the wall, in the cheap coat, the lace-trimmed crepe nightgown, just inside the lockless door. She could hear Gowan snoring in the bed, and the other men moving about, on the porch and in the hall and in the kitchen, talking, their voices indistinguishable through the door. After a while they got quiet. Then she could hear nothing at all save Gowan as he choked and snored and moaned through his battered nose and face.

She heard the door open. The man came in, without trying to be silent. He entered, passing within a foot of her. She knew it was Goodwin before he spoke. He went to the bed. "I want the raincoat," he said. "Sit up and take it off." The woman could hear the shucks in the mattress as Temple sat up and Goodwin took the raincoat off of her. He returned across the floor and went out.

She stood just inside the door. She could tell all of them by the way they breathed.

Then, without having heard, felt, the door open, she began to smell something: the brilliantine which Popeye used on his hair. She did not see Popeye at all when he entered and passed her; she did not know he had entered yet; she was waiting for him; until Tommy entered, following Popeye. Tommy crept into the room, also soundless; she would have been no more aware of his entrance than of Popeye's if it hadn't been for his eyes. They glowed, breast-high, with a profound interrogation, then they disappeared and the woman could then feel him, squatting beside her; she knew that he too was looking toward the bed over which Popeye stood in the darkness, upon which Temple and Gowan lay, with Gowan snoring and choking and snoring. The woman stood just inside the door.

She could hear no sound from the shucks, so she remained motionless beside the door, with Tommy squatting beside her, his face toward the invisible bed. Then she smelled the brilliantine again. Or rather, she felt Tommy move from beside her, without a sound, as though the stealthy evacuation of his position blew soft and cold upon her in the black silence; without seeing or hearing him, she knew that he had crept again from the room, following Popeye. She heard them go down the hall; the last sound died out of the house.

She went to the bed. Temple did not move until the woman touched her. Then she began to struggle. The woman found Temple's mouth and put her hand over it, though Temple had not attempted to scream. She lay on the shuck mattress, turning and thrashing her body from side to side, rolling her head, holding the coat together across her breast but making no sound.

"You fool!" the woman said in a thin, fierce whisper. "It's me. It's just me."

X, 140–153:

"Then she began to say 'I'll tell my father! I'll tell my father!' until I had to hold her.

" 'Get up' I says 'Will you get up and walk quiet?'

IX, 79, 3–21:

Temple ceased to roll her head, but she still thrashed from side to side beneath the woman's hand. "I'll tell my father!" she said. "I'll tell my father!"

The woman held her. "Get up," she said.

GALLEY

BOOK

" 'Will you get me out of here?' she says 'Will you? Will you?'

"When she got up she couldn't stand up, for shaking and trembling. I had to hold her up, telling her to be quiet. She got quiet. She wanted to stop and get her clothes, but I wouldn't let her. 'Do you want your clothes' I says 'or do you want to get out of here?'"

Temple ceased to struggle. She lay still, rigid. The woman could hear her wild breathing. "Will you get up and walk quiet?" the woman said.

"Yes!" Temple said. "Will you get me out of here? Will you? Will you?"

"Yes," the woman said. "Get up." Temple got up, the shucks whispering. In the further darkness Gowan snored, savage and profound. At first Temple couldn't stand alone. The woman held her up. "Stop it," the woman said. "You've got to stop it. You've got to be quiet."

"I want my clothes," Temple whispered. "I haven't got anything on but . . ."

"Do you want your clothes," the woman said, "or do you want to get out of here?"

X, 154–187

X, 188–447

X, 448–573

IX, 79, 22 — end of chapter (unchanged)

XI, 84, 1 — end of chapter (unchanged)

XII, 92, 1 — end of chapter (unchanged)

XI, 1–12 (canceled):

T memple [*sic*] heard Popeye curse Tommy and order him back down the road, and when she stood in the corner beside the shotgun, crying quietly in the dusk, she was thinking of him squatting there in the bushes beside the car; thinking of herself running down the road in the twilight, her coat streaming behind her, her ankles wrenching and lurching in the sand, until she overtook him and squatted beside him; of the two of them squatting there in the bushes until daylight. She had completely eliminated Gowan from her mind.

XI, 13–19:

She did not even look for him when she entered the diningroom, her face fixed in a cringing, placative expression. She was looking for Tommy. She went swiftly toward him, across the turned faces. Someone intervened: a hard hand and arm; she attempted to evade him, looking at Tommy.

VIII, 62, 1–8:

Temple entered the dining-room from the kitchen, her face fixed in a cringing, placative expression; she was quite blind when she entered, holding her coat about her, her hat thrust upward and back at that dissolute angle. After a moment she saw Tommy. She went straight toward him, as if she had been looking for him all the while. Something intervened: a hard forearm; she attempted to evade it, looking at Tommy.

XI, 20–525

VIII, 62, 9 — end of chapter (unchanged)

GALLEY

XI, 526–645

XII, 1–4:
"But that girl," Horace said. "You know she was all right. You know that."

The woman sat on the edge of the bed, looking down at the child.

XII, 4–7

XII, 7–25:
"That car passed me about halfway back to the house," she said in a flat, toneless voice. "She was in it. I dont know what time it was. It was about half way back to the house."

"You had turned around and were going back?"

"I forgot to bring his bottle," she said. Her hand went out and hovered about the child's face. For a time it performed those needless, brooding, maternal actions with the covers as though it responded instinctively to old compulsions of habit and care while the discretion of the mind slept. Then she sat again, her hands quiet in her lap, her face bent above the child. "So I had to go back. Lee was in our room. He came to the door and looked at me and I said 'Yes. What. What is it.' About noon the car came and he sent word for the sheriff."

BOOK

XIII, 96, 1 — end of chapter (unchanged)

XIX, 156, 1–7:
"But that girl," Horace said. "She was all right. You know she was all right when you left the house. When you saw her in the car with him. He was just giving her a lift to town. She was all right. You know she was all right."

The woman sat on the edge of the bed, looking down at the child.

XIX, 158, 6–9 (unchanged)

XIV, 100, 1 — end of chapter:
While she was sitting beside the spring, with the sleeping child upon her knees, the woman discovered that she had forgot its bottle. She sat there for about an hour after Popeye left her. Then she returned to the road and turned back toward the house. When she was about halfway back to the house, carrying the child in her arms, Popeye's car passed her. She heard it coming and she got out of the road and stood there and watched it come dropping down the hill. Temple and Popeye were in it. Popeye did not make any sign, though Temple looked full at the woman. From beneath her hat Temple looked the woman full in the face, without any sign of recognition whatever. The face did not turn, the eyes did not wake; to the woman beside the road it was like a small, dead-colored mask drawn past her on a string and then away. The car went on, lurching and jolting in the ruts. The woman went on to the house.

The blind man was sitting on the front porch, in the sun. When she entered the hall, she was walking fast. She was not aware of the child's thin weight. She found Goodwin in their bedroom. He was in the act of putting on a frayed tie; looking at him, she saw that he had just shaved.

"Yes," she said. "What is it? What is it?"

"I've got to walk up to Tull's and telephone for the sheriff," he said.

"The sheriff," she said. "Yes. All right." She came to the bed and laid the

GALLEY   BOOK

child carefully down. "To Tull's," she said. "Yes. He's got a phone."

"You'll have to cook," Goodwin said. "There's Pap."

"You can give him some cold bread. He wont mind. There's some left in the stove. He wont mind."

"I'll go," Goodwin said. "You stay here."

"To Tull's," she said. "All right." Tull was the man at whose house Gowan had found a car. It was two miles away. Tull's family was at dinner. They asked her to stop. "I just want to use the telephone," she said. The telephone was in the dining-room, where they were eating. She called, with them sitting about the table. She didn't know the number. "The Sheriff," she said patiently into the mouthpiece. Then she got the sheriff, with Tull's family sitting about the table, about the Sunday dinner. "A dead man. You pass Mr Tull's about a mile and turn off to the right. . . . Yes, the Old Frenchman place. Yes. This is Mrs Goodwin talking . . . Goodwin. Yes."

XII, 26–94 (canceled):

Each time he passed the jail he would find himself looking up at the window, to see the hand or the wisp of tobacco smoke blowing along the sunshine. The wall was now in sunlight, the hand lying there in sunlight too, looking dingier, smaller, more tragic than ever, yet he turned his head quickly away. It was as though from that tiny clot of knuckles he was about to reconstruct an edifice upon which he would not dare to look, like an archaeologist who, from a meagre sifting of vertebrae, reconstructs a shape out of the nightmares of his own childhood, and he looked quickly away as the car went smoothly on and the jail, the shabby purlieus of the square gave way to shady lawns and houses—all the stability which he had known always—a stage upon which tragedy kept to a certain predictableness, decorum.

Of course she's all right, he said. She's down there at school now. Probably just gotten over being thoroughly scared, damn her. Damn her. They passed the final fringe of cabins and small houses like the fraying

hem of a garment, and the final filling-sta-
tion—that fatuous and optimistic dream of
man in which the apotheosis of his indolence
sits at the roadside, grinding coins out of a
spigot furnished him gratis and with the very
upkeep of which he need not concern himself. "Of course she's all right," he said.
"Things like that dont happen."

"Sir?" Isom said.

"What? Oh, nothing. Nothing." The
fields were stoutly green with young cotton
and corn. Now and then men and animals,
tiny with distance, moved among the rows in
the level afternoon. Against patches of woods
already darkening into the virile green of full
summer the dogwood was almost gone, less
than a stain. Only the locust was still in
bloom, in ragged foam above the green tunnel of the drive. When they turned in at the
gate the scent of it was heavy on the air and
at every breath it snowed down the sunny
vista and lay diffident snow upon the packed
cinders.

"Things like that dont happen," he said.
"This is a civilised age, say what you want
to."

"Yes," Miss Jenny said. "I've heard
that."

"It's when I think of Little Belle; think
that at any moment . . ." Against the book
on the table the photograph sat under the
lamp. Along the four edges of it was the
narrow imprint of the missing frame. The
face wore an expression of sweet and bemused self-consciousness. The short hair
was straight and smooth, neither light nor
dark; the eyes darker than light and with a
shining quality beneath soft and secret lids;
a prim smooth mouth innocently travestied
by the painted bow of the period. He began
to whisper Damn him, damn him, tramping
back and forth before the photograph.

In the window the faint curtains moved in
shadowy peristalsis upon the smooth belly of
the dark. The darkness was shrill with the
drowsy dissonance of early summer cicadas,
and with darkness the scents of the garden
seemed to have increased tenfold, permeant,
corruptive, and he thought of that afternoon

99

last fall when he had first watched Gowan walking there in the garden, impeccable, decorous, plumply cavalier.

XII, 95–103:

"He came out to the kitchen while I was getting breakfast," the woman said. "Wild looking, with his face all bloody and swollen. I tried to get him to wash it off, but he kept on jabbering about her until I made him understand she was down there in the crib asleep, then he calmed down some and said he was going to get a car. I told him where the nearest one was, and he wouldn't even wait for breakfast."

X, 81, 1 — 82, 21:

While the woman was cooking breakfast, the child still—or already—asleep in the box behind the stove, she heard a blundering sound approaching across the porch and stop at the door. When she looked around she saw the wild and battered and bloody apparition which she recognized as Gowan. His face, beneath a two days' stubble, was marked, his lip was cut. One eye was closed and the front of his shirt and coat were blood-stained to the waist. Through his swollen and stiffened lips he was trying to say something. At first the woman could not understand a word. "Go and bathe your face," she said. "Wait. Come in here and sit down. I'll get the basin."

He looked at her, trying to talk. "Oh," the woman said. "She's all right. She's down in the crib, asleep." She had to repeat it three or four times, patiently. "In the crib. Asleep. I stayed with her until daylight. Go wash your face, now."

Gowan got a little calmer then. He began to talk about getting a car.

"The nearest one is at Tull's, two miles away," the woman said. "Wash your face and eat some breakfast."

Gowan entered the kitchen, talking about getting the car. "I'll get it and take her on back to school. One of the other girls will slip her in. It'll be all right then. Dont you think it'll be all right then?" He came to the table and took a cigarette from the pack and tried to light it with his shaking hands. He had trouble putting it into his mouth, and he could not light it at all until the woman came and held the match. But he took but one draw, then he stood, holding the cigarette in his hand, looking at it with his one good eye in a kind of dull amazement. He threw the cigarette away and turned toward the door, staggering and catching himself. "Go get car," he said.

"Get something to eat first," the woman said. "Maybe a cup of coffee will help you."

"Go get car," Gowan said. When he crossed the porch he paused long enough to splash some water upon his face, without helping his appearance much.

XII, 104–144

X, 82, 22 — end of chapter (unchanged)

XII, 145–181 (canceled):

Damn it, it is a civilised age, Horace thought, tramping back and forth while the sweet, soft, secret face came and went beneath the cylindrical blur of highlight which the lamp cast upon the glossy surface of the portrait, [*sic*] We are civilised, no matter how hard we try not to be. The stupidity of it, of believing that evil is merely an empty sound called daring; merely a closet of shiny costumes from which you can dress yourself for an evening. It's because they are fools enough to believe that older people, grown people, are wiser than they; because they believe that they must do all the things the magazines and movies tell them are expected of young people. Teaching them that the courageous thing is to live your own life, when nobody has an own life at sixty, let alone sixteen. "Damn him, damn him," he whispered, tramping back and forth before the photograph.

If we'd just let them alone, he thought, thinking of the potential evil in everyone, even children; thinking of Temple back at school, spending perhaps one sleepless night in which for a little while and for the first time since she was born, she had completely forgot herself. Not over one night, he said. Then she'll realise that she has escaped and then it'll be a whispered tale over a box of candy, probably clumped pinpoints of cigarettes in the secure dark and soft gasps and crowding surges under fleeting silk, like puppies in a basket, five or six in the bed. But to think that by merely existing, drawing breath, they should be at the mercy of such . . ." [*sic*] 'Damn him," he whispered, "damn him," tramping back and forth while the soft, bemused face blurred and faded in and out of the photograph.

XII, 182–213:

The curtains billowed steadily and faintly, as though to the shrill pulsing of the cicadas, and he thought how darkness is that agent which destroys the edifice with which light shapes people to a certain predictable behavior, as though by the impact of eyes; thinking of the grape arbor, of the murmur of young voices darkening into silence and into the pale whisper of Little Belle's small white dress, of the delicate and urgent mammalian whisper of that curious small flesh in which was vatted delicately a seething sympathy of the blossoming grape. He drew a chair to the table and moved the photograph until the face was clear of the highlight, gazing at the sweet, veiled enigma. As though there were in events a fatality which takes its color from the minds privy to the events, he thought. As though a disaster not a part of the plan could be engendered by his lack of concern and my fundamental pessimism and her furious woman's desire for retributive justice. . . . He rose quickly, the chair scraping on the floor. Again the face blurred into the highlight, yet the familiarity of the face's planes enabled him still to see it, as though beneath disturbed water or through steam, and he looked down at the face with a sort of still horror and despair, at a face more blurred than sweet, at eyes more secret than soft. He reached for it so quickly that he knocked it flat, whereupon once more the face mused tenderly behind the rigid travesty of the painted mouth.

XIX, 162, 8 — 163, 7:

He returned to town. The night was warm, the darkness filled with the sound of new-fledged cicadas. He was using a bed, one chair, a bureau on which he had spread a towel and upon which lay his brushes, his watch, his pipe and tobacco pouch, and, propped against a book, a photograph of his step-daughter, Little Belle. Upon the glazed surface a highlight lay. He shifted the photograph until the face came clear. He stood before it, looking at the sweet, inscrutable face which looked in turn at something just beyond his shoulder, out of the dead cardboard. He was thinking of the grape arbor in Kinston, of summer twilight and the murmur of voices darkening into silence as he approached, who meant them, her, no harm; who meant her less than harm, good God; darkening into the pale whisper of her white dress, of the delicate and urgent mammalian whisper of that curious small flesh which he had not begot and in which appeared to be vatted delicately some seething sympathy with the blossoming grape.

He moved, suddenly. As of its own accord the photograph had shifted, slipping a little from its precarious balancing against the book. The image blurred into the highlight, like something familiar seen beneath disturbed though clear water; he looked at the familiar image with a kind of quiet horror and despair, at a face suddenly older in sin than he would ever be, a face more blurred than sweet, at eyes more secret than soft. In reaching for it, he knocked it flat; whereupon once more the face mused tenderly behind the rigid travesty of the painted mouth, contemplating something beyond his shoulder.

XII, 214–237 (canceled):

The hall was dark. In moccasins his feet made no noise. Though slowing, the initial impulse carried him halfway down the stairs before he stopped, one hand on the balustrade, his head and shoulders still in that faint diffusion of light from the transom above Miss Jenny's door, remembering the extension of the telephone in Miss Jenny's room, telling

himself that the reason was that he did not
want to disturb her, knowing that the reason
was that he did not want even Miss Jenny to
know what an old woman he was. But the real
reason was that he was afraid to face in the
darkness what he might find at the other end
of the wire.

He turned and mounted the stairs and
tapped at Miss Jenny's door. She bade him
enter and he found her reading in bed. In the
shadow beside the bed the cot presented an
unbroken surface, ridged in a faint curve.

"Dont get tangled in the cord," Miss
Jenny said. One end of it was tied to the bed-
post beside her head, the other end disappeared at the top of the ridge of bedclothing
on the cot. "Did you dream who committed
the murder?"

XIX, 160, 9–23 (new):

"But that girl," Horace said. "She was
all right. When you were coming back to the
house the next morning after the baby's bottle, you saw her and knew she was all right."
The room gave onto the square. Through the
window he could see the young men pitching
dollars in the courthouse yard, and the wagons passing or tethered about the hitching
chains, and he could hear the footsteps and
voices of people on the slow and unhurried
pavement below the window; the people buying comfortable things to take home and eat
at quiet tables. "You know she was all
right."

That night Horace went out to his sister's
in a hired car; he did not telephone. He
found Miss Jenny in her room. "Well," she
said. "Narcissa will—"

"I dont want to see her," Horace said.

XII, 238–287

XIX, 160, 23 — 162, 7 (unchanged)

XII, 288–303 (canceled):

In his room again he stood at the window,
feeling the dark soft whisper of the curtains
against his cheek. Invisible, stirred seem-
ingly by the cicadas, since there was scarce
any movement of the darkness itself; the
cicadas become now a drowsy sound, numb-
ing, almost pleasant, as prolonged disso-

nance does. There was no movement, yet
the body of night, darkness, was filled with
that yawning sense of teeming and accomplished space. The window looked south.
Four miles of peaceful night lay between,
yet he believed that he could see the glow of
town low in the sky; dark flat shapes of roof-
lines; a square building with dim grated
window, a pale blob of knuckles motionless
in one of the interstices.

XII, 304–314:

It was three o'clock when he passed the
jail on foot and looked up at the window. It
was empty: an orderly checker-boarding of
pale squares in a blank wall under the low
morning star. The square was empty, the
air chill with dawn. He moved in echoing
isolation beneath the lighted face of the clock
on the courthouse and the sparse lights which
filled the doorways and niches in the blank
facades of stores with shadows in humped
shapes like ranks of patient vultures.

XII, 315–331:

The station was still three quarters of a
mile away. The waiting-room, lit by a single
dirt-crusted globe, was empty save for a man
in overalls sprawled on his back, his head
on a folded coat, snoring, and a woman in a
calico dress, a dingy shawl and an awkward
hat bright with rigid and moribund flowers,
her head bent and her hands crossed on a
paper-wrapped parcel on her lap, a straw
suit-case at her feet. He discovered then
that he had forgotten the book. The photograph was still propped against it—the very
thing which had driven him from bed to walk
four and three quarters miles in the darkness—and his inner eye showed it to him
suddenly, blurred by the highlight, and beside it his freshly loaded pipe. He searched
his coat again, finding only the pouch.

XII, 332–460

XII, 461–470 (canceled):
Watching them Horace began to laugh, without mirth. And this is what I have been
losing sleep over, he thought. What can a
creature like that suffer, else where the dig-

XIX, 163, 7–10:
He lay in bed, dressed, with the light burning, until he heard the courthouse clock
strike three. Then he left the house, putting
his watch and his tobacco pouch into his
pocket.

XIX, 163, 11–20:
The railroad station was three quarters
of a mile away. The waiting room was lit
by a single weak bulb. It was empty save for
a man in overalls asleep on a bench, his
head on his folded coat, snoring, and a woman
in a calico dress, in a dingy shawl and a new
hat trimmed with rigid and moribund flowers
set square and awkward on her head. Her
head was bent; she may have been asleep;
her hands crossed on a paper-wrapped parcel upon her lap, a straw suit case at her
feet. It was then that Horace found that he
had forgot his pipe.

XIX, 163, 21 —— 167, 8 (unchanged)

nity in tragedy—that one quality which we do not possess in common with the beasts of the field, standing there in the bright dappling of noon, thinking that she might have been the very one who forced him to step off the walk in order to pass her: the supreme gesture of that irony which ordered his life.

XII, 471–620

XIX, 167, 9 — 171, 10 (unchanged)

XII, 620–635 (canceled):
But once more the man went out of his mind and he was thinking of the jail window, of the hand lying in it; of the woman. Tell me again about that girl.

She was in the car. It passed me about halfway back to the house. I dont know what time it was. He was going fast, rough road and all, and I thought then about how he was going to get around that tree. She looked at me when they passed. Just looked at me. She didn't wave or anything. She just looked at where I was standing when they passed. Her hat was on crooked, like it was last night, and I thought then that when she put it on that morning in the kitchen it was on straight, but I just thought that . . .

XII, 636–733

XIX, 171, 11 — end of chapter (unchanged)

XII, 734–744 (canceled):
Isom was at the station, with the car. When they crossed the square the lighted clock-hands stood at half past eight. He looked up at the hotel wall and leaned forward suddenly. "I want to stop at the hotel a minute, Isom."

The drummers sat along the curb, with cigars and cigarettes; across the way and a little further down the street the barred window of the jail was empty beneath the ragged shadow of the tree, and there were no figures leaning along the fence any more.

XX, 174, 1–17 (new):
As Horace was leaving the station at Jefferson a townward-bound car slowed beside him. It was the taxi which he used to go out to his sister's. "I'll give you a ride this time," the driver said.

"Much obliged," Horace said. He got in. When the car entered the square, the court-

GALLEY

BOOK

house clock said only twenty minutes past eight, yet there was no light in the hotel room window. "Maybe the child's asleep," Horace said. He said, "If you'll just drop me at the hotel—" Then he found that the driver was watching him, with a kind of discreet curiosity.

"You been out of town today," the driver said.

"Yes," Horace said. "What is it? What happened here today?"

"She aint staying at the hotel anymore. I heard Mrs Walker taken her in at the jail."

"Oh," Horace said. "I'll get out at the hotel."

GALLEY	BOOK
XII, 745–809	*XX, 174, 18 — 176, 20 (unchanged)*
XIII, 1–501	*XVIII, 132, 1 — 145, 29 (unchanged)*
XIV, 1–278	*XVIII, 146, 1 — 153, 13 (unchanged)*
XV, 1–69	*XVIII, 153, 14 — end of chapter (unchanged)*
XVI, 1–371	*XXI, 182, 1 — end of chapter (unchanged)*
XVII, 1–48	*XX, 180, 21 — end of chapter (unchanged)*

XVII, 49–58:

When he reached home on his return from Oxford he said: "Well, I guess I'll have to take her to the house, now. By God, when I think of those— If there'd just been a man. But you cant hit a damned doddering old he-goat. I swear, I believe it was that hotel man did it. I dont believe even a Baptist woman would . . ." Then he became aware that his sister was speaking. She had not looked up from the magazine on her lap.

XX, 176, 20–22:

On the next afternoon Horace went out to his sister's, again in a hired car. He told her what had happened. "I'll have to take her home now."

XVII, 59–86

XX, 176, 23 — 177, 16 (unchanged)

XX, 177, 17–30 (new):

She rose. "Will you stay here tonight?"

"What? No. No. I'll—I told her I'd come for her at the jail and . . ." He sucked at his pipe. "Well, I dont suppose it matters. I hope it doesn't."

She was still paused, turning. "Will you stay or not?"

"I could even tell her I had a puncture," Horace said. "Time's not such a bad thing after all. Use it right, and you can stretch anything out, like a rubberband, until it

GALLEY

BOOK

busts somewhere, and there you are, with all tragedy and despair in two little knots between thumb and finger of each hand."

"Will you stay, or wont you stay, Horace?" Narcissa said.

"I think I'll stay," Horace said.

XVII, 87–122:

When he went to his room he packed the suitcase again. He went to bed. He lay tossing in the darkness, laughing now and then with savage mirthlessness. He thought of Temple. He thought of her floating in a canoe under the Michigan moon, with a ukelele perhaps, and an entranced and fatuous male leaning across the paddle toward the studiedly consonantless sound of her voice. Then he thought of the woman again, lying yonder at the jail, on the charity of the keeper of a house of public detention, where the authorities would doubtless not permit her to stay. He thought of himself before them, facing them across a smug table, saying Gentlemen, give me the key to that cell and I'll solve your problem in ten minutes, and unsully your fair city beyond fear of repetition and dread of recourse. Then he began to laugh again, writhing slowly, the sheets becoming unbearable with the temperature of his impotent rage.

The door opened. He lifted his head, looking across the black footboard into the black darkness where the door had yawned, felt rather than seen or heard. His sister spoke.

"Horace."

"Yes?" He rose to his elbow. He could hear her garments, then she took shape, vaguely. "Look out for the bag," he said. "I dont remember where I left it. So it's probably where it can be stumbled over with the minimum of effort."

"I see it." She approached and stood beside the bed, looking down at him, solidifying into that immobility which was a part of all her movements, passing from attitude to attitude with that tranquillity of pagan statuary.

XVII, 123–189

XX, 177, 31 — 178, 4:

He was in bed. He had been lying in the dark for about an hour, when the door of the room opened, felt rather than seen or heard. It was his sister. He rose to his elbow. She took shape vaguely, approaching the bed. She came and looked down at him.

XX, 178, 5 — 179, 28 (unchanged)

GALLEY   BOOK

XVII, 189–206 (canceled):
He followed the sound of her garments with
his eyes. The door yawned again.

The shrill darkness leaned steadily upon
the curtains. I'm going to Europe, Horace
said. Soon as this business is finished.
This damned country. I'll write Belle for a
divorce and—he lay for a tense moment,
then he started to swing his feet to the floor,
but refrained. I'll write tomorrow. I
couldn't even write a sane letter to anyone
now.

When he went down to breakfast he carried
the bag with him. She and the boy were at
the table.

"Are you going in this morning?" she
said.

"Yes. I'll be closer to my work. I hope
to be too busy from now on to change my
mind anymore."

She poured his coffee.

XX, 179, 29 (new):
The next morning at breakfast, his sister
said:

XVII, 206–221:
"Who will be on the other side of the case?
    "District Attorney. Why?"
She rang the bell. The pantry door opened.
"Bring Mr Horace some hot bread, Isom."
Horace was still watching her. "Why did
you ask that? I never knew you to ask an idle
question before. . . . Damn little squirt,"
he said. "I swear, I believe he was at the
bottom of that, last night. Getting her turned
out of the hotel for public effect, political
capital. By God, if I knew he did a thing like
that just to get elected to Congress . . . When
there's not a member of the bar in the state
can bawl louder about the sanctity of the
home, motherhood . . ." [Also see Galley
XXII, 74–92, below.]

XX, 179, 29 — 180, 20:
"Who will be the lawyer on the other side of
the case?"
    "District Attorney. Why?"
She rang the bell and sent for fresh bread.
Horace watched her. "Why do you ask that?"
Then he said: "Damn little squirt." He was
talking about the District Attorney, who had
also been raised in Jefferson and who had
gone to the town school with them. "I believe he was at the bottom of that business
night before last. The hotel. Getting her
turned out of the hotel for public effect, political capital. By God, if I knew that, believed
that he had done that just to get elected to
Congress . . ."

After Horace left, Narcissa went up to
Miss Jenny's room. "Who is the District
Attorney?" she said.

"You've known him all your life," Miss
Jenny said. "You even elected him. Eustace
Graham. What do you want to know for?
Are you looking around for a substitute for
Gowan Stevens?"

"I just wondered," Narcissa said.

GALLEY

BOOK

"Fiddlesticks," Miss Jenny said. "You dont wonder. You just do things and then stop until the next time to do something comes around."

XVII, 222–315

XXII, 193, 1 — 196, 4 (unchanged)

XVII, 316–321 (canceled):

But not in this house, Horace said, his mind flicking here and there while the voice still lingered in his ear with that nameless portent, thinking of the implements which evil employed and of the implements with which it had to be combatted.

XVII, 322–448

XXII, 196, 5 — end of chapter (unchanged)

XVII, 449–465 (canceled):

When he had gone Horace entered the house and turned on the light, blinking after the subtle treachery of the moon. Little Belle's photograph sat on the mantel. He took it down, looking at it. The light hung on a shadeless cord, low; the shadow of his body lay upon the photograph. He moved it so that the light fell upon it, then drew it back into the shadow again. The difference was too intangible to discern, even by its own immediate comparison; the white still white, the black still black, the secret, musing expression unaltered. Delicate, evocative, strange, looking up out of the shadow with a crass brazenness, a crass belief that the beholder were blind. He set it back on the mantel and sat down and wrote the letter to Belle in Kentucky, offering a divorce.

XVIII, 1–556

XXIII, 200, 1 — 215, 20 (unchanged)

XVIII, 557–565:

He found the light and turned it on. Belle's letter was propped on the mantel. He took it up and looked at the superscription, at the small disfigurations which held a name, a juxtaposition of letters which did not move him at all, scrawled there by a hand that had no actual relation to his life, feeling the hard ball of coffee inside him.

Then he was looking at the photograph, holding it in his hands.

XVIII, 565–602

XXIII, 215, 21–22:

He found the light and turned it on. The photograph sat on the dresser. He took it up, holding it in his hands.

XXIII, 215, 23 — end of chapter (unchanged)

GALLEY

BOOK

XIX, 1–619

XXIV, 217, 1 — end of chapter (unchanged)

XX, 1–240

XXV, 235, 1 — 242, 2 (unchanged)

XXI, 1–373

XXV, 242, 3 — end of chapter (unchanged)

XXII, 1–74:

XXVI, 253, 1 — 254, 19:

It was just five o'clock when he put Belle's letter into the postoffice. The sun was just about to show. But it would be two hours yet before he could get breakfast even, so he walked quietly about the town, watching it rise and wake into the increasing immaculate morning, making his plans to go abroad. He thought of Belle, then he was thinking of the three of them. He saw Belle and Narcissa and the woman with the child on her lap, all sitting on the cot in the jail, and himself like one of those furious and aimless bugs that dart with sporadic and unbelievable speed upon the surface of stagnant water as though in furious escape from the very substance that spawned them, as he strove with subterfuge and evasion and stubbornness and injustice, with that fundamental abhorrence of truth which is in mankind.

I'll go to Europe, he said. I'm sick. I'm sick to death. Looking about him he saw his life isolated in all its ludicrous and optimistic frustration; looking ahead he could see it diminishing into a small frenzied dust where he strove with the subterfuge and prejudice and lying, to no end. What did it matter who killed the man? what became of Goodwin, of her, of a fool little girl, of himself? All that matters is to accomplish what is in hand, clean up the mess he had got himself into, then be forever afterward as fearful as any buck of the scent or sight or sound of collective man.

The first thing would be to clean up the mess. He would sub-poena Temple; he thought in a paroxysm of raging pleasure of flinging her into the court-room, of stripping her: This is what a man has killed another over. This, the offspring of respectable people: let them blush for shame, since he could never blush for anything again. Stripping her, background, environment, all. Not that it mattered whether they hung Goodwin or not, any more than it mattered whether or

When the sun rose, Horace had not been to bed nor even undressed. He was just finishing a letter to his wife, addressed to her at her father's in Kentucky, asking for a divorce. He sat at the table, looking down at the single page written neatly and illegibly over, feeling quiet and empty for the first time since he had found Popeye watching him across the spring four weeks ago. While he was sitting there he began to smell coffee from somewhere. "I'll finish this business and then I'll go to Europe. I am sick. I am too old for this. I was born too old for it, and so I am sick to death for quiet."

He shaved and made coffee and drank a cup and ate some bread. When he passed the hotel, the bus which met the morning train was at the curb, with the drummers getting into it. Clarence Snopes was one of them, carrying a tan suit case.

"Going down to Jackson for a couple of days on a little business," he said. "Too bad I missed you last night. I come on back in a car. I reckon you was settled for the night, maybe?" He looked down at Horace, vast, pasty, his intention unmistakable. "I could have took you to a place most folks dont know about. Where a man can do just whatever he is big enough to do. But there'll be another time, since I done got to know you better." He lowered his voice a little, moving a little aside. "Dont you be uneasy. I aint a talker. When I'm here, in Jefferson, I'm one fellow; what I am up town with a bunch of good sports aint nobody's business but mine and theirn. Aint that right?"

Later in the morning, from a distance he saw his sister on the street ahead of him turn and disappear into a door. He tried to find her by looking into all the stores within the radius of where she must have turned, and asking the clerks. She was in none of them. The only place he did not investigate was a stairway that mounted between two

110

not Tommy was dead. Telling the jury What
ever you do will be as stupid as what has
been done, but just do something, because he
was sick to death. Then suddenly, passing a
house, he smelled coffee, and he knew he
could not do that. He went to the hotel and
with knife and fork he dug himself back into
that world he had vomited himself out of for
a time, in which he must follow a certain ordered procedure about which he had neither
volition nor will.

After breakfast he felt better. It might
not be necessary to use Temple at all. He
need only arrange to procure her if things
went wrong. Whatever he did, the evidence
against Goodwin was not strong enough to
convict him as it was now, and so when he
saw Senator Snopes on the street he was
almost civil to him. Snopes was sitting before the hotel, a bag at his feet.

"Going down to Jackson for a couple of
days," he said. "Too bad I missed you the
other night. I could have took you to a place
most folks dont know about, where a man
can do anything he's big enough to do. I
reckon there'll be another time, though. And
dont you be uneasy none. I aint no talker.
When I'm in Jefferson I'm one thing; when
I'm up town aint nobody's business but mine.
And I expect to treat everybody the same
way."

That day he met his sister on the street.
They talked for a few minutes, then parted.
She went on and turned and mounted a nar-
row stairway between two stores.

XXII, 74–92 (canceled):
The day Horace moved back to town, when
Miss Jenny came down Narcissa said:

"He's gone back to town. He thinks he
ought to be nearer his client."

"I gathered that from the way he went to
bed last night," Miss Jenny said. "Why dont
you let him alone until he gets done with his
case? He'll go on home then."

"I know it," Narcissa said. "Who is the
District Attorney?"

"You've known him all your life. Eustace
Graham. Dont you remember reading about

stores, to a corridor of offices on the first
floor, one of which was that of District Attorney Eustace Graham.

it in the paper when he got elected last winter?"

"No, I dont remember."

"What do you think about while you are
reading the paper, then?"

"Eustace Graham," Narcissa said. "Yes.
I know him."

XXII, 93–107:

He had a club foot. As usual, the defor-
mity had invested him in the eyes of the town
with that sentimental illusion of deserving
worth. That boy'll get somewhere, they
said, simply because he drove a grocery
wagon and then a truck with a club foot—the
one in which the foot could be neither help
nor hindrance, the other in which it was an
asset. He got as far as the state university,
where he played poker each Saturday night
in the office of a livery stable. When he
graduated in law he left an anecdote behind
him.

It was in the poker game. The bet came
to him. He looked across at the proprietor,
who was his only remaining opponent.

XXVI, 254, 20 — 255, 18:

Graham had a club foot, which had elected
him to the office he now held. He worked
his way into and through the State University; as a youth the town remembered him as
driving wagons and trucks for grocery
stores. During his first year at the University he made a name for himself by his industry. He waited on table in the commons
and he had the government contract for
carrying the mail to and from the local postoffice at the arrival of each train, hobbling
along with the sack over his shoulder: a
pleasant, open-faced young man with a word
for everyone and a certain alert rapacity
about the eyes. During his second year he
let his mail contract lapse and he resigned
from his job in the commons; he also had a
new suit. People were glad that he had
saved through his industry to where he could
give all his time to his studies. He was in
the law school then, and the law professors
groomed him like a race-horse. He graduated well, though without distinction. "Because he was handicapped at the start," the
professors said. "If he had had the same
start that the others had . . . He will go
far," they said.

It was not until he had left school that
they learned that he had been playing poker
for three years in the office of a livery
stable, behind drawn shades. When, two
years out of school, he got elected to the
State legislature, they began to tell an anecdote of his school days.

It was in the poker game in the livery
stable office. The bet came to Graham. He
looked across the table at the owner of the
stable, who was his only remaining opponent.

XXII, 108–225

XXVI, 255, 19 — 258, 25 (unchanged)

GALLEY

BOOK

XXII, 225–235:

XXVI, 258, 25 — end of chapter:

When a jew lawyer can hold up an American, a white man, and not give him but ten dollars for something that two Americans already give him ten times that much for something exactly like it, we need a law. I been a liberal spender all my life; whatever I had has always been my friends', but when a durn, stinking, lowlife—"

"Why'd you sell it to him, then?" a barber said.

"What?" Snopes said. ". . . Have a cigar?"

When a jew lawyer can hold up an American, a white man, and not give him but ten dollars for something that two Americans, Americans, southron gentlemen; a judge living in the capital of the State of Mississippi and a lawyer that's going to be as big a man as his paw some day, and a judge too; when they give him ten times as much for the same thing than the lowlife jew, we need a law. I been a liberal spender all my life; whatever I had has always been my friends' too. But when a durn, stinking, lowlife jew will refuse to pay an American one tenth of what another American, and a judge at that—"

"Why did you sell it to him, then?" the barber said.

"What?" Snopes said. The barber was looking at him.

"What was you trying to sell to that car when it run over you?" the barber said.

"Have a cigar," Snopes said.

XXIII, 1–35:

XXVII, 260, 1 — 262, 6:

TZ he [*sic*] trial opened on the twentieth of June. On the table lay the sparse objects which the District Attorney had offered in evidence: the bullet from Tommy's skull, a stoneware jug half full of corn whisky.

Horace had not summoned Temple. Twice he had telephoned Miss Reba, the second time two days before the trial opened.

"They aint here no more," Miss Reba said. "I dont know nuttin about them and I dont want to know nuttin."

"But cant you find where she went to, in case I need her?"

"I dont know nuttin and I dont want to," Miss Reba said. Thank God, Horace said, thank God. He realized now that it was too late, that he could not have summoned her; realized again that furious homogeneity of the middle classes when opposed to the proletariat from which it so recently sprung and by which it is so often threatened. Better that he should hang, he thought, than to expose . . . than to expose . . . I cannot even face the picture, he told himself.

"I will call Mrs Goodwin to the stand,"

The trial was set for the twentieth of June. A week after his Memphis visit, Horace telephoned Miss Reba. "Just to know if she's still there," he said. "So I can reach her if I need to."

"She's here," Miss Reba said. "But this reaching. I dont like it. I dont want no cops around here unless they are on my business."

"It'll be only a bailiff," Horace said. "Someone to hand a paper into her own hand."

"Let the postman do it, then," Miss Reba said. "He comes here anyway. In a uniform too. He dont look no worse in it than a full-blowed cop, neither. Let him do it."

"I wont bother you," Horace said. "I wont make you any trouble."

"I know you aint," Miss Reba said. Her voice was thin, harsh, over the wire. "I aint going to let you. Minnie's done took a crying spell tonight, over that bastard that left her, and me and Miss Myrtle was sitting here, and we got started crying too. Me and Minnie and Miss Myrtle. We drunk up a whole new bottle of gin. I cant afford that.

GALLEY

he said. He did not look around, but he felt Goodwin's eyes come to rest quickly upon him. He could feel them as he helped the woman into the chair and while she was being sworn. With the child on her lap she began her testimony, repeating the story as she had told it to him in the hotel that morning the child was ill. Twice Goodwin tried to interrupt and was silenced. Horace could feel the cold fury of his gaze, but he would not look around.

BOOK

So dont you be sending no jay cops up here with no letters for nobody. You telephone me and I'll turn them both out on the street and you can have them arrested there."

On the night of the nineteenth he telephoned her again. He had some trouble in getting in touch with her.

"They're gone," she said. "Both of them. Dont you read no papers?"

"What papers?" Horace said. "Hello. Hello!"

"They aint here no more, I said," Miss Reba said. "I dont know nuttin about them and I dont want to know nuttin except who's going to pay me a week's room rent on—"

"But cant you find where she went to? I need her."

"I dont know nuttin and I dont want to know nuttin," Miss Reba said. He heard the receiver click. Yet the disconnection was not made at once. He heard the receiver thud onto the table where the telephone sat, and he could hear Miss Reba shouting for Minnie: "Minnie. Minnie!" Then some hand lifted the receiver and set it onto the hook; the wire clicked in his ear. After a while a detached Delsarte-ish voice said: "Pine Bluff dizzent . . . Enkyew!"

The trial opened the next day. On the table lay the sparse objects which the District Attorney was offering: the bullet from Tommy's skull, a stoneware jug containing corn whiskey.

"I will call Mrs Goodwin to the stand," Horace said. He did not look back. He could feel Goodwin's eyes on his back as he helped the woman into the chair. She was sworn, the child lying on her lap. She repeated the story as she had told it to him on the day after the child was ill. Twice Goodwin tried to interrupt and was silenced by the Court. Horace would not look at him.

XXIII, 36–56

XXIII, 57–62:

   "I waive, your Honor," the District Attorney said, glancing at the jury. Damn! Horace thought. He took me then.

   When court adjourned for the day Good-

XXVII, 262, 6 — 262, 25 (unchanged)

XXVII, 262, 26–30:

   "I waive, your Honor," the District Attorney said, glancing at the jury.

   When court adjourned for the day Goodwin said bitterly: "Well, you've said you would

win said bitterly: "Well, you've said you would kill me someday, but I didn't think you meant it."

kill me someday, but I didn't think you meant it. I didn't think that you—"

XXIII, 63–114

XXVII, 262, 31 — 264, 10 (unchanged)

XXIII, 115–122:

Horace returned to the front, breathing deep to clear his lungs and his nostrils. He returned to town, to the jail. They admitted him. He mounted the stairs; the jailer locked a door behind him. Through the barred window of the general room he could see the windows in the hotel wall, thinking of the fatality which may be engendered by a conviction of disaster.

XXVII, 264, 11–13:

Horace returned to town, to the jail. They admitted him. He mounted the stairs; the jailer locked a door behind him.

XXIII, 123–205

XXVII, 264, 14 — 266, 23 (unchanged)

XXIII, 206–208:

Horace began to construct the scene, coaching the woman, pausing now and then to tramp back and forth upon the narrow floor.

XXVII, 266, 24–25:

Horace began to drill the woman, tramping back and forth upon the narrow floor.

XXIII, 209–221

XXVII, 266, 25 — 267, 5 (unchanged)

XXIII, 222–224:

The clocks struck eleven. Still Horace drilled her, going over and over the imaginary scene, trying to anticipate every eventuality.

XXVII, 267, 6–7:

The clock struck eleven. Still Horace drilled her, going over and over the imaginary scene.

XXIII, 224–247

XXVII, 267, 7–28 (unchanged)

XXIII, 247–250:

Can you stupid mammals never believe that any man, every man—" he began to flap his hands in a faint repressed gesture.

XXVII, 267, 28–29:

Can you stupid mammals never believe that any man, every man—

XXIII, 250–262

XXVII, 267, 29 — 268, 8 (unchanged)

XXIII, 262–267:

I told you we didn't have—"

"Oh, Lord; oh, Lord; oh, Lord," Horace whispered.

"If that aint enough pay, I don't know that I blame you."

XXVII, 268, 8–10:

I told you we didn't have—If that aint enough pay, I don't know that I blame you."

XXIII, 268–280

XXVII, 268, 11–22 (unchanged)

XXIII, 281–289:

She looked at him, her eyes grave and blank and contemplative, and they looked at one another across that old barrier composed on the one hand of a quixotic folly which she knows serenely will soon be com-

XXVII, 268, 23–24:

She looked at him, he eyes grave and blank and contemplative. Outside the clock struck twelve.

pletely lost in the recrudescent fury of the flesh; on the other hand of a cold despair which he knows sorrowfully that the immemorial magic of the flesh will anneal. Outside the clock struck twelve.

XXIII, 290–491

XXIII, 491–519:
Horace stopped, motionless. A jew, he said. A jew lawyer, his glance flicking away, darting this way and that about the adjacent heads. For seconds before he saw Temple he knew what he was going to find.

Once when he was a boy he had two possums in a barrel. A negro told him to put a cat in with them if he wanted to see something, and he had done so. When he could move at all he ran to his mother in a passion of crying that sent him staggering and vomiting toward the house. All that night he lay beneath an ice-pack in a lighted room, tearing himself now and then by main strength out of writhing coil of cat-entrails, toward the thin, shawled figure of his mother sitting beside the bed.

"Mr Benbow," the Court was saying, "this is your witness?"

"It is, your Honor."

"You wish her sworn?"

"Yes, your Honor," he heard himself saying, while all the time it seemed to him that he still heard the bell ringing and the bailiff's voice on the balcony beneath the eaves where the pigeons preened and crooned:

"The honorable Circuit Court of Yoknapatawpha County is now open according to law. . . ."

XXIV, 1–239

XXV, 1–83 (canceled):

June 23.
"Dear Narcissa—

"I ran. Once I had not the courage to admit it; now I have not the courage to deny it. I found more reality than I could stomach, I suppose. Call it that, anyway. I dont seem to care. Only I wish Belle had stayed in Kentucky. At least, that's out of the whole

XXVII, 268, 25 — 274, 17 (unchanged)

XXVII, 274, 17 — end of chapter:
Horace stopped just within the door. "It's a lawyer," he said. "A Jew lawyer from Memphis." Then he was looking at the backs of the heads about the table, where the witnesses and such would be. "I know what I'll find before I find it," he said. "She will have on a black hat."

He walked up the aisle. From beyond the balcony window where the sound of the bell seemed to be and where beneath the eaves the gutteral pigeons crooned, the voice of the bailiff came:

"The honorable Circuit Court of Yoknapatawpha County is now open according to law. . . ."

Temple had on a black hat. The clerk called her name twice before she moved and took the stand. After a while Horace realised that he was being spoken to, a little testily, by the Court.

"Is this your witness, Mr Benbow?"

"It is, your Honor."

"You wish her sworn and recorded?"

"I do, your Honor."

Beyond the window, beneath the unhurried pigeons, the bailiff's voice still droned, reiterant, importunate, and detached, though the sound of the bell had ceased.

XXVIII, 276, 1 — end of chapter (unchanged)

damned state where such things can happen.

"She was at home. When Jones—you remember him: the one who says he used to
lead Kinston society; now he drives it—put
me down at the corner, I saw her shade up
and the rosy light, and I thought of that unfailing aptitude of women for coinciding with
the emotional periphery of a man at the
exact moment when it reaches top dead center, at the exact moment when the fates have
prized his jaws for the regurgitated bit.
Thus (your own words) like a nigger I left
her; like a nigger I returned (via the kitchen);
entered the house and stood in the door while
she laid her magazine down and watched me
from her pink nest while I shed the ultimate
cockleburr of errant itch and the final mud-
flake of the high pastures where the air had
been a little too ardent and a little too stark,
and so into the old barn and the warm twilight and the old stall fitting again to the
honorable trace-galls, and, ay, the old man-
ger lipped satin-smooth by the old unfailing
oats.

"Little Belle is not at home. Thank God:
at what age does man cease to believe he
must support a certain figure before his
women-folks? She is at a house-party.
Where, Belle did not say, other than it di-
vulging to be in the exact center of bad telephone connections. Thank God she is no
flesh and blood of mine. I thank God that no
bone and flesh of mine has taken that form
which, rife with its inherent folly, knells and
bequeaths its own disaster, untouched. Untouched, mind you. That's what hurts. Not
that there is evil in the world; evil belong
[*sic*] in the world: it is the mortar in which
the bricks are set. It's that they can be so
impervious to the mire which they reveal
and teach us to abhor; can wallow without
tarnishment in the very stuff in the comparison with which their bright, tragic,
fleeting magic lies. Cling to it. Not through
fear; merely through some innate instinct of
female economy, as they will employ any
wiles whatever to haggle a butcher out of a
penny. Thank God I have not and will never
have a child—and for that reason I have as-

117

sailed not only a long distance, but a rural,
line at eleven P.M. in order to hear a cool,
polite, faintly surprised young voice on an
unsatisfactory wire; a voice that, between
polite inanities in response to inanities,
carried on a verbal skirmishing with another
one—not feminine—without even doing me the
compliment of trying to conceal the fact that
she had been squired to the telephone; needs
must project over the dead wire to me,
whose hair she has watched thinning for ten
years, that young mammalian rifeness which
she discovered herself less long ago than I
the fact that, [*sic*] to anyone less than twenty-
five years old, I am worse than dead.

"I ran. I dont try to palliate it. But I
want to rectify it as far as possible. I know
this will be distasteful to you, but it will be
the last time, I promise that; next time I
may not even have the courage to return. I
want you to find that woman yourself; tell
her that I must give up the case because I do
not think I am good enough, and that I am
putting it in the hands of the best criminal
lawyer I can find, for an appeal, and that she
is not to worry. Do this, my dear. You will
have no trouble finding her. She's there now,
in front of the jail with that child, standing
where he can see them from the window:
have I not seen her there a thousand times?
God, if he were the only one who had to see
her there now.

"Horace."

XXVI, 1–21 (canceled):

"June 29.

"Dear Horace—

"I received your letter. Your message
to that woman I cut off and mailed to her at
the jail. I imagine she got it. They took the
man away the day after you left. They were
getting ready to lynch him, some said. So
Jefferson is spared that at least. Why they
should want to I cant see, since they are
going to hang him anyway. So you can save
hiring another lawyer.

"Bory has been quite sick. Sundy will let
him eat green fruit. A nigger is the ruin of
any white child. I dont know what to do. I
cant say anything, because Miss Jenny is so

118

GALLEY

BOOK

foolish about the darkies. She is as usual.
She sends love.

"I am glad to hear you have decided to
stay at home after this. I think that is wise.
Belle is only thirty-eight. She might not be
three [*sic*] when you come back, next time.

"Love,

"Narcissa."

XXIX, 284, 1 — end of chapter (new)

XXX, 290, 1 — end of chapter (new)

XXVII, 1–9:

While on his way to Pensacola to visit his
mother, Popeye was arrested in Birmingham for the murder of a policeman in a
small Alabama town on the night of June 17,
1929. At that time he was sitting in a parked
touring car near a Memphis road-house, and
he said "For Christ's sake," looking about
the cell in the county jail, his free hand
finicking a cigarette from his coat.

XXXI, 294, 1–7:

While on his way to Pensacola to visit his
mother, Popeye was arrested in Birmingham for the murder of a policeman in a
small Alabama town on June 17 of that year.
He was arrested in August. It was on the
night of June 17 that Temple had passed him
sitting in the parked car beside the road
house on the night when Red had been killed.

XXXI, 294, 8 — 302, 7 (new):

Each summer Popeye went to see his
mother. She thought he was a night clerk in
a Memphis hotel.

His mother was the daughter of a board-
ing house keeper. His father had been a
professional strike-breaker hired by the
street railway company to break a strike in
1900. His mother at that time was working
in a department store downtown. For three
nights she rode home on the car beside the
motorman's seat on which Popeye's father
rode. One night the strike-breaker got off
at her corner with her and walked to her
home.

"Wont you get fired?" she said.

"By who?" the strike-breaker said.
They walked along together. He was well-
dressed. "Them others would take me that
quick. They know it, too."

"Who would take you?"

"The strikers. I dont care a damn who
is running the car, see. I'll ride with one as
soon as another. Sooner, if I could make
this route every night at this time."

She walked beside him. "You dont mean
that," she said.

"Sure I do." He took her arm.

"I guess you'd just as soon be married to one as another, the same way."

"Who told you that?" he said. "Have them bastards been talking about me?"

A month later she told him that they would have to be married.

"How do you mean, have to?" he said.

"I dont dare to tell them. I would have to go away. I dont dare."

"Well, dont get upset. I'd just as lief. I have to pass here every night anyway."

They were married. He would pass the corner at night. He would ring the foot-bell. Sometimes he would come home. He would give her money. Her mother liked him: he would come roaring into the house at dinner time on Sunday, calling the other clients, even the old ones, by their first names. Then one day he didn't come back; he didn't ring the foot-bell when the trolley passed. The strike was over by then. She had a Christmas card from him; a picture, with a bell and an embossed wreath in gilt, from a Georgia town. It said: "The boys trying to fix it up here. But these folks awful slow. Will maybe move on until we strike a good town ha ha." The word, strike, was underscored.

Three weeks after her marriage, she had begun to ail. She was pregnant then. She did not go to a doctor, because an old Negro woman told her what was wrong. Popeye was born on the Christmas day on which the card was received. At first they thought he was blind. Then they found that he was not blind, though he did not learn to walk and talk until he was about four years old. In the meantime, the second husband of her mother, an undersized, snuffy man with a mild, rich moustache, who pottered about the house—he fixed all the broken steps and leaky drains and such—left home one afternoon with a check signed in blank to pay a twelve dollar butcher's bill. He never came back. He drew from the bank his wife's fourteen hundred dollar savings account, and disappeared.

The daughter was still working down-

town, while her mother tended the child.
One afternoon one of the clients returned
and found his room on fire. He put it out; a
week later he found a smudge in his waste-
basket. The grandmother was tending the
child. She carried it about with her. One
evening she was not in sight. The whole
household turned out. A neighbor turned in
a fire alarm and the firemen found the
grandmother in the attic, stamping out a fire
in a handful of excelsior in the center of the
floor, the child asleep in a discarded mattress nearby.

"Them bastards are trying to get him,"
the old woman said. "They set the house on
fire." The next day, all the clients left.

The young woman quit her job. She
stayed at home all the time. "You ought to
get out and get some air," the grandmother
said.

"I get enough air," the daughter said.

"You could go out and buy the groceries," the mother said. "You could buy them
cheaper."

"We get them cheap enough."

She would watch all the fires; she would
not have a match in the house. She kept a
few hidden behind a brick in the outside wall.
Popeye was three years old then. He looked
about one, though he could eat pretty well. A
doctor had told his mother to feed him eggs
cooked in olive oil. One afternoon the gro-
cer's boy, entering the area-way on a bicy-
cle, skidded and fell. Something leaked
from the package. "It aint eggs," the boy
said. "See?" It was a bottle of olive oil.
"You ought to buy that oil in cans, anyway,"
the boy said. "He cant tell no difference in
it. I'll bring you another one. And you want
to have that gate fixed. Do you want I should
break my neck on it?"

He had not returned by six oclock. It was
summer. There was no fire, not a match in
the house. "I'll be back in five minutes,"
the daughter said.

She left the house. The grandmother
watched her disappear. Then she wrapped
the child up in a light blanket and left the
house. The street was a side street, just off

121

a main street where there were markets, where the rich people in limousines stopped on the way home to shop. When she reached the corner, a car was just drawing in to the curb. A woman got out and entered a store, leaving a Negro driver behind the wheel. She went to the car.

"I want a half a dollar," she said.

The Negro looked at her. "A which?"

"A half a dollar. The boy busted the bottle."

"Oh," the Negro said. He reached in his pocket. "How am I going to keep it straight, with you collecting out here. Did she send you for the money out here?"

"I want a half a dollar. He busted the bottle."

"I reckon I better go in, then," the Negro said. "Seem like to me you folks would see that folks got what they buy, folks that been trading here long as we is."

"It's a half a dollar," the woman said. He gave her a half dollar and entered the store. The woman watched him. Then she laid the child on the seat of the car, and followed the Negro. It was a self-serve place, where the customers moved slowly along a railing in single file. The Negro was next to the white woman who had left the car. The grandmother watched the woman pass back to the Negro a loose handful of bottles of sauce and catsup. "That'll be a dollar and a quarter," she said. The Negro gave her the money. She took it and passed them and crossed the room. There was a bottle of imported Italian olive oil, with a price tag. "I got twenty-eight cents more," she said. She moved on, watching the price tags, until she found one that said twenty-eight cents. It was seven bars of bath soap. With the two parcels she left the store. There was a policeman at the corner. "I'm out of matches," she said.

The policeman dug into his pocket. "Why didn't you buy some while you were there?" he said.

"I just forgot it. You know how it is, shopping with a child."

"Where is the child?"

"I traded it in," the woman said.

"You ought to be in vaudeville," the policeman said. "How many matches do you want? I aint got but one or two."

"Just one," the woman said. "I never do light a fire with but one."

"You ought to be in vaudeville," the policeman said. "You'd bring down the house."

"I am," the woman said. "I bring down the house."

"What house?" He looked at her. "The poor house?"

"I'll bring it down," the woman said. "You watch the papers tomorrow. I hope they get my name right."

"What's your name? Calvin Coolidge?"

"No, sir. That's my boy."

"Oh. That's why you had so much trouble shopping, is it? You ought to be in vaudeville. . . . Will two matches be enough?"

They had had three alarms from that address, so they didn't hurry. The first to arrive was the daughter. The door was locked, and when the firemen came and chopped it down, the house was already gutted. The grandmother was leaning out an upstairs window through which the smoke already curled. "Them bastards," she said. "They thought they would get him. But I told them I would show them. I told them so."

The mother thought that Popeye had perished also. They held her, shrieking, while the shouting face of the grandmother vanished into the smoke, and the shell of the house caved in; that was where the woman and the policeman carrying the child, found her: a young woman with a wild face, her mouth open, looking at the child with a vague air, scouring her loose hair slowly upward from her temples with both hands. She never wholly recovered. What with the hard work and the lack of fresh air, diversion, and the disease, the legacy which her brief husband had left her, she was not in any condition to stand shock, and there were times when she still believed that the child had perished, even though she held it in her arms crooning above it.

Popeye might well have been dead. He had no hair at all until he was five years old, by which time he was already a kind of day pupil at an institution: an undersized, weak child with a stomach so delicate that the slightest deviation from a strict regimen fixed for him by the doctor would throw him into convulsions. "Alcohol would kill him like strychnine," the doctor said. "And he will never be a man, properly speaking. With care, he will live some time longer. But he will never he any older than he is now." He was talking to the woman who had found Popeye in her car that day when his grandmother burned the house down and at whose instigation Popeye was under the doctor's care. She would fetch him to her home in afternoons and for holidays, where he would play by himself. She decided to have a children's party for him. She told him about it, bought him a new suit. When the afternoon of the party came and the guests began to arrive, Popeye could not be found. Finally a servant found a bathroom door locked. They called the child, but got no answer. They sent for a locksmith, but in the meantime the woman, frightened, had the door broken in with an axe. The bathroom was empty. The window was open. It gave onto a lower roof, from which a drain-pipe descended to the ground. But Popeye was gone. On the floor lay a wicker cage in which two lovebirds lived; beside it lay the birds themselves, and the bloody scissors with which he had cut them up alive.

Three months later, at the instigation of a neighbor of the mother, Popeye was arrested and sent to a home for incorrigible children. He had cut up a half-grown kitten the same way.

His mother was an invalid. The woman who had tried to befriend the child supported her, letting her do needlework and such. After Popeye was out—he was let out after five years, his behavior having been impeccable, as being cured—he would write to her two or three times a year, from Mobile and then

New Orleans and then Memphis. Each summer he would return home to see her, prosperous, quiet, thin, black, and uncommunicative in his narrow black suits. He told her that his business was being night clerk in hotels; that, following his profession, he would move from town to town, as a doctor or a lawyer might.

While he was on his way home that summer they arrested him for killing a man in one town and at an hour when he was in another town killing somebody else—that man who made money and had nothing he could do with it, spend it for, since he knew that alcohol would kill him like poison, who had no friends and had never known a woman and knew he could never—and he said, "For Christ's sake," looking about the cell in the jail of the town where the policeman had been killed, his free hand (the other was handcuffed to the officer who had brought him from Birmingham) finicking a cigarette from his coat.

XXVII, 10–224

XXXI, 302, 8 — 308, 9 (unchanged)

XXVII, 225–266

XXXI, 308, 12 — end of chapter (unchanged)

XXVII, 267–268:

    Sure, the sheriff said, I'll fix it for you; springing the trap.

XXXI, 308, 10–11:

    "Sure," the sheriff said. "I'll fix it for you"; springing the trap.

Lightning Source UK Ltd.
Milton Keynes UK
UKOW05f1105310715

256086UK00006B/129/P

9 780292 769052